HOW TO ACCELERATE WEALTH ON ANY INCOME

The Road To Mastering Money Management

G. Michael Cocoris, CFS

Interior and exterior design by John T. Cocoris

**To my wife, Patricia,
who is a wonderful wife, my best friend,
a gracious lady, a good teacher
and a great master of personal
money management.**

TABLE OF CONTENTS

PREFACE

My first experience with managing money came at the young age of 13. My mother, who had been divorced from my father for many years, decided that I, as the elder son, should help her manage the household finances. Shortly thereafter, while still in junior high school, I went to work and began managing my own money. While my mother did the best she could with her limited income, when I graduated from high school, I had no other option but to work my way through college and seminary. I was so broke, I wore the same pair of shoes every day for seven years.

Over many years, using the advice of others and personal experience, I learned how to manage money. In the 1950s, when I was a teenager, I opened a savings account. At the time, it was all I knew to do. In the 1960s, I took out several cash-value life insurance policies and purchased a rental unit. In the 1970s, several of my friends and I went together to purchase a house to fix up and resell. In the 1980s, when interest rates hit double digits, I took my money out of my savings account and put it into a money market account that was paying 16%+ interest. At that rate, it did not take long to double what I was making on my money. I also put money in an annuity and an oil investment. In the 90s, I put money in mutual funds and several private placements. I have also purchased stocks.

My interest in money matters goes beyond my personal experience. I have spent virtually my entire adult life in the ministry. Years ago, I discovered that money was a major problem in many marriages. In 1975, I began speaking in family conferences across the United States on, among other things, family finances. I have served on the boards of six non-profit organizations, including a college and a university. Through these experiences of counseling as a minister and serving as a board member, I saw the great need for a simple course in personal money management.

In 1993, I began putting together a financial seminar. That provoked me to seek professional training. I obtained a life and disability insurance license in California and a stockbroker's security license (Series 7). I have worked at a regional office of a national life insurance company and managed a financial planning office. I have also earned the financial designation of CFS (Certified Fund Specialist), which is specialized training in various types of funds, including mutual funds, annuities, educational funds, and retirement funds. I am a graduate of the Online Trading Academy, an intensive day-trading course.

I have also spent decades studying the Scriptures. I have discovered that the principles of money management taught by professionals are reflected in the Bible.

My wife, Patricia, who also obtained an insurance and a securities license, and I have taught a financial seminar titled "How to Accumulate Wealth on Any Income." By the way, she not only typed this manuscript, but she also provided many helpful suggestions.

What follows is a course in personal money management. It covers many areas of finance, including insurance, buying a house, taxes, investments, and estate planning. It should be noted that I have not had a license to sell property and casualty insurance, that is, insurance on property such as a home and a car. I have not been an accountant, a real estate broker, or an attorney. I have had professionals in those fields review that material in this course.

My purposes are 1) to clearly explain the basic concepts of personal money management, 2) to point out along the way that the Bible reflects the principles of personal money management, 3) to show how the principles of personal money management work together, and 4) to provide suggestions for how you can begin to implement these principles. These purposes are strictly educational. *They are not to provide insurance, investment, accounting, tax, or legal advice on any particular situation for the simple reason that every situation is different. For such advice, a competent professional should be consulted.*

I owe Teresa Rogers many thanks for graciously proofreading the manuscript.

My goal is to guide you through a process to help you learn to manage your money and reach your financial goals.

G. Michael Cocoris, CFS
Santa Monica, CA

Chapter 1

YOU CAN ACCUMULATE WEALTH!

You need to accumulate wealth. If you have not already purchased a house, you need to save money for a down payment. If you have children, you need to set aside money to cover college costs. You need to invest now so you will have enough for retirement.

You also need to accumulate wealth to have money to give. Solomon wrote, "A good *man* leaves an inheritance to his children's children" (Proverbs 13:22). Obviously, not all have children or grandchildren, but the point is that it is a good thing to manage your money so that you have money to give! Jesus said, "It is more blessed to give than to receive" (Acts 20:35). Paul wrote, "Let him who stole steal no longer, but rather let him labor, working with *his* hands what is good, that he may have something to give him who has need" (Eph. 4:28).

You need to accumulate wealth and you can. Yes, you. Regardless of your income, if you follow sound, well-established financial principles, you can amass wealth. Others have done it and so can you.

The word "accumulate" is chosen with care. It means "to collect, gather, to increase in number." It implies a *process*. No get-rich-quick schemes will be recommended here. Instead, there is a procedure to follow for building, preserving, and even passing on wealth.

The term "wealth" is also selected carefully. It means "abundance of resources." It conveys the idea of an ample quantity, a relative degree of plentifulness. Nothing here guarantees you will become a millionaire, although, under some circumstances, that is possible. Instead, if the process suggested is followed, barring some unforeseen tragedy, you should be able, over time, to accumulate not only more than enough for you to retire comfortably but also enough to leave money to others you love.

The Problem

Why is it that more middle-income Americans in this land of opportunity do not amass more wealth? For starters, if you are like most middle-income Americans, you have never received adequate instruction concerning managing your money. From your parents, you probably heard, "Do not waste money" or "Save some of your money." School, including high school and college, taught you little, if anything, about how to handle money. As an adult, someone may have given you advice on a particular financial issue like buying a car, purchasing a house, obtaining insurance, or even given you a hot tip on an investment, but you, like the vast majority, have probably never been taught even the most basic principles of personal money management.

The consequences of not knowing and, thus, failing to follow sound principles of money management are unfortunate. Due to a lack of knowledge and/or discipline, some get so deep in debt that they end up in foreclosure or bankruptcy. Others do not go that far, but they have such large debts that they pay hundreds and thousands of dollars in interest. Then, some do not get into deep debt. They manage to live on what they earn, with perhaps a small manageable debt. They might have a few dollars in savings, but not much; they have never accumulated much wealth. Few arrive at retirement age financially independent. That is unfortunate because it is unnecessary. You *can* learn how to accumulate wealth no matter what your income level.

The Solution

In a sense, the solution is simple. Yet, to those who have never been taught or who know some of the concepts and have not practiced them, the solution can be difficult.

Information If at least part of the problem is a lack of instruction, part of the solution is information. What follows is designed to teach the basic principles of money management. Mastering how to manage money is the key to maximizing money and amassing wealth. This material covers personal finance, including saving, budgeting, credit, insurance, home ownership, taxes, investments, retirement planning, and estate planning.

Admittedly, some of the material is fundamental, especially at the beginning. It is common sense, but it is necessary to cover even the simplest concepts for the simple reason that common sense is not common. What may be simple or common sense to one may be a revelation to another. After talking in depth with people about their personal finances for years, I have learned not to take anything for granted.

Implementation If you are to learn how to master money management and thereby accumulate wealth, you must not only know the concepts in each of the areas of personal finance, but you must also be able to implement and practice them. For that reason, at the end of each chapter, there is an exercise called "My Action Plan." It will be tempting for some, perhaps the ones who need it the most, to read these pages with curiosity and keep going. I urge you not to do that. If, and only if, you are already *practicing* the principles in an area or if, for some reason, you do not need the suggestions, of course, there is no need for you to go through the exercise. Otherwise, you should, as much as possible, complete the action plan at the end of each section. Information alone will not enable you to manage money. Insight alone will not empower you to accumulate wealth. Only action will accomplish what you really desire, namely, to manage your money and amass some degree of wealth for retirement, etc.

Perhaps it should be added that the process might even be painful. For those who have been undisciplined in their financial affairs and consequently gotten themselves into debt, it might even be *very* painful, but as has been said many times, "If there is no pain, there is no gain." Whatever your financial situation, apart from inheriting a fortune or winning the lottery, if you are to reach your financial goals, you must be willing to pay the price.

Investments The goal is to master money management so you can save enough money to invest. Then your money will be working for you, helping you accumulate wealth *even faster*. There are many ways to invest, including bank accounts, real estate, insurance (surprised?), tangible assets, and, of course, securities such as money markets, bonds, stocks, and mutual funds. These will be discussed in more detail later.

The reason that investments enable you to accumulate wealth faster is the principle of compound interest. It has been suggested that "The greatest power on earth is the power of compound interest." Compound interest is earning interest on on both the principal and the *previous interest* earned. Interest can be compounded annually, semi-annually, quarterly, and daily.

To illustrate the concept, suppose you invested $1000 in an investment earning 10% a year. (10% is used to illustrate the concept. In any given year, 10% may be unrealistically high.) In the first year, you would earn $100 (1000 x 10% = 100), bringing your total to $1100. In the second year, you would earn $110 (1100 x 10% = $110), bringing the total to $1210. In the third year, you would earn $121 (1210 x 10% = 121), for a total of $1331. As you can see, the same original investment of $1000 earns more and more every year because after the first year, you are not only earning interest on the principal of $1000, but you are also earning interest on the interest earned on the $1000.

For the principle to work for you, you must invest and continuously reinvest the interest earned. In addition, the longer the time compound interest has to work, the greater the return. In other words, if you invest a small sum of money and reinvest what you make in interest, over time, you will make a very large sum of money, especially if you do it tax-deferred.

If you saved $1.43 a day and put it in a can in the backyard, you would *save* $5219.90 in 10 years, but if you saved $1.43 a day and *invested* it every year in a tax-deferred account, such as an Individual Retirement Account (an IRA), earning 10%, you would have $10,399.04 in 10 years. That's the power of compound interest!

Earning interest can actually double your money. How long it takes to double depends on the interest rate being earned. The rule of 72 states that if you divide an interest rate by 72, the result will be the number of years it will take for the original investment to double. To say the same thing another way, 72 divided by the interest rate equals the number of years it takes for an investment to double. For example, any amount invested earning 10% will double in 7.2 years. (72 divided by 10 equals 7.2.) The following chart shows how long it takes money to double at various interest rates.

72	÷	Interest rate	=	Years
72	÷	12%	=	6.0
72	÷	10%	=	7.2
72	÷	8%	=	9.0
72	÷	6%	=	12.0
72	÷	4%	=	18.0

When you graduated from high school at age 18, if you had invested $9,370.41 in a tax-deferred account earning 10% compound interest and never added another dime, at age 67 (your current Social Security retirement age), you would have $1,000,000 in the account! If you waited until after college graduation to accumulate $1,000,000 in a retirement account at age 67, you would have to invest $13,719.21. If you waited until you were 30, you would need to put $29,408.35 into the retirement account.

The problem is that you did not have $9,370.41 when you graduated from high school or $13,719.21 when you graduated from college. So let's look at a more realistic example.

When you graduated from high school at age 18, if you put $2,000 a year ($166.66 a month) into the tax-deferred retirement account *every year* until you were 67, you would have $3,134,175.88 in the account. If you waited until after you graduated from college, you would have $2,096,500.34 waiting for you at age 67. If you waited until you were 30, you would have $931,965.94 in your tax-deferred retirement account.

Remember those oil wells you have seen in fields beside the road? Like seesaws, they move up and down, up and down, up and down. They work 24 hours a day, seven days a week. Until they retire, they never take a break, call in sick, or take a vacation. They just work and work and work and work. You need your money to work for you like that.

First, you must have some money you can use to begin the process, but ultimately, you need money working for you as hard as you work for it. Actually, someday, you'll need your money working for you, so that you *do not* need to be working for it.

Summary: If you have the knowledge, discipline, and desire to implement sound financial principles, you can accumulate wealth and have it work for you rather than you working for it. The issue is not the amount of money you make. It is having discernment, direction, daily discipline, dogged determination, and ultimately a deep desire.

Years ago, a newspaper reporter wrote a story on a football player who made $4 million in salary and bonuses. In court papers, the football player said that he was broke and could not pay his bills. The reporter quoted a stockbroker who said, "You think it's hard to blow $4 million in four years? I have seen a player go through $30,000 in six weeks at a versatiler. You try to restrict their spending, and they fire you."

Without desire and discipline, any financial situation is hopeless, but if you have the desire and are willing to discipline yourself to apply the principles you are about to read, there is hope, hope that you, yes, even you, can accumulate wealth regardless of your income.

Chapter 2

GET ON THE ROAD

All right, let's get started. If the objective is to accumulate wealth, where should you begin? There are several different answers to that question. Your answer will depend on your current financial situation. If you are deep in debt, you will probably say that before you can do anything, you must get out of debt. A case can be made for that approach. If you have little or no debt, you might suggest that the place to start is saving so you can invest. Not a bad idea at all. If you have already saved some money and want to accumulate more, you are likely looking for an investment that will help you do that.

Admittedly, where *you* begin depends on where you are financially right now, but let's start at the beginning. This might be a review for you, but you may pick up some pointers.

To get on the road to successful money management, you must start saving. Even lowly ants know that they must save for the winter. Solomon suggested, "Go to the ant, you sluggard! Consider her ways and be wise, which, having no captain, overseer or ruler, provides her supplies in the summer, a*nd* gathers her food in the harvest" (Proverbs 6:6-8). Children should be taught to save. According to the Scripture, spiritual leaders are to have children who are not accused of dissipation (Titus 1:6). The Greek word rendered "dissipation" means "unable to save," hence, "wasting one's money on pleasure, wasteful." Parents are to teach their children to save money.

How much should you save? When should you start?

Begin Saving

Save Money How much should you save? The traditional answer for many, many years has been that people should save 10%.

Think of how much you would have in a savings account if you had saved 10% since you first went to work. If you had made an average of $30,000 a year for the last ten years, you would have made $300,000. If you had saved 10% of $300,000, you would have $30,000 in the bank, not counting interest that could make that figure substantially higher. If you had saved that $30,000 by putting aside $250 a month for ten years and invested it at 8%, you would have had $45,321. (This illustration does not take taxes and possible investment expenses into consideration. Nevertheless, such is possible because there are tax-deferred investment instruments and it is possible to earn 8% after expenses.)

If you are not saving 10%, you should be. If you absolutely cannot afford to save 10% at the moment, you should either: 1) reduce your expenses, or 2) save a smaller percentage and gradually increase it until you reach 10%.

You should save until you have six months of living expenses in a liquid account. If you and your spouse are both working, three months' living expenses in such an account might be sufficient. Some financial advisers recommend that, if you are self-employed, you should have a year's living expenses in this account.

This fund is your reserved account, sometimes called an "emergency fund." It should be used only in an emergency, and if any portion is used, it should be replaced as soon as possible. Once your reserved account has three months, six months, or one year of living expenses, you should begin investing the amount you are saving (hopefully 10%).

Pay Yourself First Most only save if they have something left over after they have paid all their bills. That is a mistake. Pay yourself first. If, for spiritual reasons, you are committed to giving first, pay yourself after you give. Those who begin this practice usually discover that they do not miss the money they are saving, and, even more surprisingly, they have the same amount left over as before they started saving.

Why not Now?

The objections to starting the accumulation process by saving are usually: 1) "I'm in debt. So I need to pay off my debts first." 2) "I have no discretionary money. I cannot afford it."

"I need to pay off my debts first." The case for paying off debts before attempting to save seriously is that the debts are costing a great deal in interest. The argument is that you would save money by paying off the debts.

Frankly, that is a great argument—on paper. There is simply no question that mathematically, it makes sense to say that you will save money by paying off your debts first. For example, the interest rate on credit card debt is much higher than any interest on a savings account or even a money market account.

The problem with that approach is that for many people, it simply does not work. In some cases, it is because the habit of using credit cards is so ingrained that the addicted debtor never breaks the habit. In other cases, emergencies arise, and with no money in a savings account to fall back on, the only alternative is to take on more debt. So, even though you have debt, you should consider starting a savings program *before* all your debts are paid. There are advantages to doing this. For one thing, you will have a reserved account to fall back on that can actually prevent you from increasing the debt load. Perhaps, more importantly, you will be developing a new habit that is critical to the overall program of mastering money management to accumulate wealth.

Imagine a backyard overgrown with weeds. To transform it into a beautiful lawn with a huge tree in the middle, you might conclude that all the weeds must be removed first. That plan has merit. However, a case could be made for clearing a small space in the middle of the yard, planting a tree there, and, as time permits, eliminating the remaining weeds. This approach gives the tree time to grow and provides you with the psychological satisfaction of seeing something positive happen, rather than pulling at the weeds.

"I cannot afford it." The objection that says "I have no extra money to save" is certainly legitimate. Nevertheless, every attempt should be made to start saving something. Perhaps some expenses could be eliminated, like cigarettes. A smoker once told me that he figured out how much money he would have had if he had quit smoking years ago. It was enough to buy a new sports car!

Pointedly, you should save something. If you cannot save 10%, save 5%, or 1%. If you cannot save 1%, save ½%. If any percentage is too big a bite out of your budget, select a specific amount, say $5.00 a month. If you cannot save $5.00 a month, save $1.00 a month. If you cannot save a dollar, save a quarter. If you cannot save a quarter, save pennies. Over 200 years ago, one of our wise founding fathers said, "A penny saved is a penny earned." Benjamin Franklin was right. The point is if you are ever going to get ahead financially, you must learn to save money. Why not start now?

Summary: To begin accumulating wealth, start a savings program and pay yourself first.

In 1926, George S. Clason wrote a book entitled *The Richest Man in Babylon.* It is an imaginary story set in the ancient city of Babylon, the richest city in the world at the time. The story begins with Bansir, the chariot builder, musing over the fact that Babylon consists of a "mixture of grandeur and squalor, of dazzling wealth and direst poverty."

While he was meditating, his best friend, the musician

Kobbi, dropped by to borrow some money! Bansir was broke; he had no money to loan to his friend. Together they concluded, "We are weary of being without gold in the midst of plenty. We wish to become men of means." So they decided to ask Arkad, an old friend, how he became so wealthy. Arkad started like them: "Working, Working! Getting nowhere," and now he claimed to be the richest man in Babylon.

Arkad told them that he had learned how to accumulate wealth from a very wealthy man who told him, "I found the road to wealth when I decided that a part of all I earned was mine to keep. If you did keep for yourself one-tenth of all you earn, how much would you have in ten years?" At that point, it hit Arkad that if he had done that, he would have "as much as I earn in one year."

There is more to this story. The rest of the story will be told later, but for now, the vitally important lesson that is so foundational to accumulating wealth is the old principle that you must learn to put 10% of what you earn in a liquid account.

MY ACTION PLAN: PUTTING SAVINGS INTO FOCUS

From your own experience, let's put savings into focus.

Step 1: Focus on What you could have Saved

To calculate how much you would have if you had saved 10%, follow these steps.

How many years have you worked? _____

What has been your average monthly income? _____

How much have you earned? (See the chart below.) _____

You should have saved 10% of your total earnings. _____

(This chart does not include interest earned on your savings,which would make the total much higher.)

Step 2: Calculate What you *can* Save

From the chart, figure what you can save in the future.

Years Worked	Average Monthly Income						
	$1,000	**$1,500**	**$2,000**	**$2,500**	**$3,000**	**$4,000**	**$5,000**
5	60,000	90,000	120,000	150,000	180,000	240,000	300,000
10	120,000	180,000	240,000	300,000	360,000	480,000	600,000
15	180,000	270,000	360,000	450,000	540,000	720,000	900,000
20	240,000	360,000	480,000	600,000	720,000	960,000	1,200,000
25	300,000	450,000	600,000	750,000	900,000	1,200,000	1,500,000
30	360,000	540,000	720,000	900,000	1,080,000	1,440,000	1,800,000
35	420,000	630,000	840,000	1,050,000	1,260,000	1,680,000	2,100,000

Chapter 3

STAY ON THE ROAD

Assuming you have set up a savings account, are systematically putting money into it, and are not regularly taking money out of it, the critical next step is to manage spending. You must control spending and spend wisely. To save 10% consistently, you must properly manage the remaining 90% to ensure *you save without interruption.* This is essential. If you can manage your spending, you will be a long way down the road to mastering money management, and you will be more likely to stay on the road to wealth accumulation. If you cannot live within your means, that is, within the 90% you have left after saving 10%, you will never accumulate wealth. As has been pointed out, "When your outgo exceeds your income, your upkeep is your downfall."

To manage spending, plan your spending. Centuries ago, Solomon observed, "The plans of the diligent *lead* surely to plenty, but *those of* everyone *who is* hasty, surely to poverty" (Proverbs 21:5). Jesus used planning for spending as an illustration of a spiritual truth of discipleship. He said, "For which of you, intending to build a tower, does not sit down first and count the cost, whether he has *enough* to finish *it*" (Luke 14:28).

Plan Your Spending

The spending plan is called a budget. Struggling with a budget is not new; it dates back to the Roman Empire. Roman housewives seldom received a regular allowance from their husbands each week or month. Consequently, they were forced to be very cautious in their spending. This led to the practice of keeping money for household expenses in little leather bags, each holding a sum set aside for a specific item. This custom also prevailed among businessmen who may have borrowed it from their wives or vice versa. *Bulga*, the Latin word for "bag," became attached to the careful planning of one's finances. Adopted into French as *bougette*, it eventually entered English as budget.

You should have a budget. A budget is more than a record of how much money is coming in and where your money is going. *Bookkeeping* is a record of what was spent or a list of bills that need to be paid every month. A *budget* determines what will be spent, meaning that no more will be spent than what is in the budget. To many, that sounds restrictive. To them, the very word "budget" sounds like being put in a straitjacket. Actually, the exact opposite is closer to the truth. Not having a budget or not having a proper budget usually leads to bondage, bondage to higher and higher debt payments, financial pressure, worry, arguments over money among married couples, etc. Building a realistic budget using common sense and financial data can free you from such bondage.

For a short time, my brother and I ran a custom clothing business. In dealing with a professional athlete, we discovered that, although many athletes make hundreds of thousands of dollars, they still live on a budget! We sold a suit to an athlete who made major bucks playing ball. When we concluded the deal, he could not pay us without going through his accountant! Everything was budgeted. Now, if people who make six or seven-figure incomes need a budget, so do you.

The way to design a realistic budget is covered in detail in the action plan at the end of the chapter.

Spend according to Your Plan

Having a plan and living by it are two different things. Here are some suggestions to help you live according to your plan and, beyond that, save money.

The issue is not how much or how little you make. The issue is to live within your means. You and your spouse need to agree on a budget and stick to it. Money issues can cause divorce. A budget you both agree to and stick to could save your marriage!

Do not be like the fellow who said, "Living on a budget is the same as living beyond your means, except that you have a record of it." Once you have a budget, stick to it. Set aside (or spend) the money for each item every month. Put the prorated amount for annual expenses into the savings account (see "My Action Plan" at the end of this chapter). I have even set aside the small amounts—for example, the gas allowance—by putting it in an envelope. The issue is only to spend what is in the budget. If it is not in the budget, do not buy it. Either save for it or put it in the budget. Ben Franklin said, "Beware of little expenses; a small leak will sink a great ship."

Spend Wisely

Managing your spending involves planning your spending by designing and sticking to a budget. It also involves spending wisely.

Save until you can pay cash. It is wise to avoid paying interest. The way to avoid interest is to pay cash. If you use a credit card, pay it off when you get the bill. Or *save* until you have the money in hand to make the purchase.

Here's how I learned this valuable lesson. Many years ago, I purchased a year-old Chevrolet for $2,000 (since then, inflation has taken its toll on the automobile market). The dealer gave me a $500 trade-in on my old Chevrolet, leaving a balance of $1,500. I borrowed the $1,500, but by the time I paid it back over three years, I'd paid almost $2,000. Because I had to borrow the money, that car cost me nearly 25% more than its market value. I decided there must be a better way.

So here's what I did. I drove that Chevrolet until it was paid for, and then, instead of trading it in for another car, I kept driving it and making car payments—this time to myself. I opened another savings account, not a "household" savings account for pro-rated annual bills (see "My Action Plan," at the end of the chapter), but another separate account I called my "car" savings account. My plan was to drive that Chevrolet until I had enough money in the bank to buy another car. I did not get to carry out the plan. When someone ran a stop sign and totaled my car, I had no choice but to purchase another car before I had enough money to pay for it.

With the money I had saved, I only had to borrow $500 for my next car. This time, I took out a one-year personal loan. It cost me $30 (interest rates on loans have also risen due to inflation). I drove that car until I had enough money in the bank to purchase the next one. I have followed that procedure for every car I have purchased since.

I use this plan for other major purchases. If we need an item of furniture, I open a savings account and start making payments into it. When I have enough money for it, then and only then, I buy it.

This system is smart in more ways than one. You not only avoid the interest, but you also earn interest on the money in the savings account. On top of that, if you have the cash, you can wait until an item is on sale. That can mean additional savings of 10-40, or even 50%. Now that is really smart!

Buy what you will use. Some spend money they have not earned to buy things they don't need to impress people they don't like. Many buy more than they will realistically use. How many men have more tools than they will ever use? We buy the higher-priced product to get bells and whistles we do not need.

I once bought a TV set with a split-screen feature that let me watch two channels at once. When I bought it, it sure seemed like a good idea, but I rarely used it. I paid extra for something I did not use and frankly did not need. Wise spending only buys what is needed or, at least, only what will be used.

Imagine having the money for all the things you bought that you did not use. If a fair-sized sum comes to mind, you really need to heed this principle.

Buy quality. Next, buy quality—it will last longer. My brother says, "It's not how much you pay, it's how many times you pay it." Cheaper may be more expensive in the long run.

When I was a young man, I decided that if I could buy a quality car, I would save money over time. It began when I heard that a Mercedes had a diesel engine that lasted 250,000-300,000 miles. I reasoned that even if I had to pay more, if it lasted longer, I would end up paying less in the long run.

In 1979, I purchased a 1968 Mercedes for $2,000. Admittedly, I got a good deal. It was worth much more. Two years later, I traded it in on a 1973 Mercedes costing $8,000, but they gave me a $4,000 trade-in on my '68. I drove the '73 for seven years. While someone else was driving it, a young man rear-ended it and totaled it. The insurance company gave me $6,000 for it. I bought a 1975 SLC for $9,500 (only $3,500 of which was out of pocket). I drove it until I had put over 100,000 miles on it. Later, I owned a 1987 Mercedes diesel until it had well over 250,000 miles.

Buy at the best price. Buy quality, but buy it at the best price. To do that: 1) wait for a sale, 2) shop for the best price, and 3) negotiate. Waiting for the sale is simple enough. Traditionally, clothing goes on sale in August and January. Do not buy a bathing suit at the beginning of the summer; buy that kind of item at the end of the season.

What if you cannot wait for the sale? Shop around for the best price. First, go to the "expensive" store(s), look over the options, decide what you want, and get the model number and price. Then, go to the discount stores for the best price on the model of your choice. Do not settle for a cheaper model. By the way, the best price may not be the lowest price. I once found the lowest price for a camera I wanted in a magazine ad from a mail-order house, but I chose to spend a few dollars more at a local camera shop because I got personal service.

Negotiate. In the January 17, 1994, earthquake, my microwave was thrown to the floor and destroyed. After looking at several places, I found the model I wanted to purchase as a replacement and continued to shop. I discovered a store that claimed they would match any price and went to even more stores. I found a fellow who would negotiate. When we finally got to his rock bottom price and I was still pressing him, he said, "I'll pay the sales tax." That did it. I bought. I saved an additional 8.25%.

Today, this kind of shopping can be done on the internet.

Summary: The next critical step toward mastering money management and accumulating wealth is managing spending. Manage spending by using a budget, paying cash, avoiding interest, only buying what you can use, and buying quality at the best price.

You can spend your money foolishly. You can spend it impulsively (and probably spend too much) with interest or for inferior goods. On the other hand, you can spend your money wisely. You can spend it when you get the best deal on quality products at the best price without paying interest.

To spend consistently and wisely over time will take decision, discipline, and dogged determination to live within your means. For many people, enough is never enough. A study conducted to determine how much income people need to attain a lifestyle they would enjoy found that those earning $30,000-$40,000 felt they needed approximately $45,000 per year to have "enough." Those earning $45,000-$55,000 felt they needed $65,000 per year, and those earning $60,000-$70,000 needed between $90,000 and $100,000! We need to decide to live within our means.

Calvin Coolidge said, "There is no dignity so impressive and no independence quite so important as living within your means." We will also need discipline and determination.

My wife claims that every child should have a wind-up watch because it has to be done every day. That is what we need: *daily* discipline and dogged determination.

MY ACTION PLAN: DESIGNING A REALISTIC BUDGET

To design a realistic budget, first, calculate your *monthly* income, then track and trim *all* expenses.

Step 1: Tally Your Average Available Monthly Income

Designing a budget begins with determining your average available monthly after-tax income. The reason for beginning with your monthly income rather than another amount, such as your weekly income, is that most bills are due monthly.

If you are paid monthly, determining your average monthly income is easy. What you are paid in your one monthly check, that is, your take-home pay, is your available monthly income for budgeting purposes.

If you are paid twice a month, figuring your available monthly income is simple: add the amounts of your two checks.

When you are paid either bi-weekly (every two weeks) or weekly, finding your average available monthly income is a little more involved. If you are paid bi-weekly, you get 26 paychecks a year instead of 24 as you would if you were paid twice a month. That means you receive two "extra" paychecks per year that you have to calculate. So, if you are paid bi-weekly, multiply your bi-weekly check by 2.167.

If you are paid weekly, you receive four "extra" paychecks per year. To determine your available monthly income, multiply your weekly paycheck by 4.333.

Of course, if you have two incomes (husband and wife), both amounts need to be included in the average available monthly income. Also, additional income from other sources should be included in the final total.

Step 2: Track all Expenses

Next, list all expenses in monthly terms. Regular monthly expenses include giving, saving, housing, food, transportation, insurance, debts, and entertainment.

Periodic expenses are quarterly, semiannual, and annual. These costs, such as clothing, property taxes, some insurance bills, vacations, Christmas presents, and gifts throughout the year, should be prorated. Divide the total *annual* expenditure by 12 and add that amount to the monthly budget. The prorated amount for each item can be set aside in a savings account every month. When a quarterly, semiannual, or annual bill comes due, the funds are available in the "prorated account" to pay it. For example, if you have children, you have to buy school clothes every fall. If you try to pay for that annual expense out of that month's paycheck, you may discover it is impossible. So you charge that expense, paying interest for months to come for the privilege. The solution is to prorate the expense and set aside the required amount each month. You may have to work your way into the prorated system. You might have to begin by putting a lump sum from your savings into it, or if you are paid bi-weekly or weekly, by putting one of those "extra" checks into it.

I prorate income taxes (that is, self-employed people pay income taxes and social security tax quarterly), property taxes, house insurance, car insurance, money for a car, and money for furniture. I also add a little more than necessary to each amount. If a particular item costs $1000 per year, the monthly prorated amount is $83.33. I round it off at $84, $85, or $90. That way, I save a little extra money.

Daily cash expenses should also be included. A budget must include *all* expenses, even goof-off money. Any item not in the budget is a potential budget buster. To ensure you have everything within your budget, you should track all expenditures for one month. Record all cash expenditures daily and all other expenses weekly.

See the worksheet at the end of this action plan.

Step 3: Trim your Expenditures

After you have an accurate record of all expenditures, trim non-essentials and spending until your budget approximates the general guidelines of a standard budget and/or your particular goals and dreams. A standardized budget has approximate percentages for various items in a family budget. There is no "right" budget for everyone. Your budget should reflect your unique income, needs, and preferences. These percentages may be unsuitable for your situation at the moment. Nevertheless, a standardized budget will give you budgeting guidelines that are important for qualifying for a home loan. A standard budget of after-tax money looks something like this:

Giving	10%
Saving	10%
Housing	30%
Food	15%
Transportation	10%
Clothing	5%
Medical	5%
Insurance	5%
Vacation/Recreation	5%
Miscellaneous	5%

When you get a raise, adjust your budget. You control your budget and, until you change it for a valid reason, it should control your normal spending.

A realistic budget that includes all expenditures, even goof-off money, is not restrictive; it is a path to financial freedom. Instead of bondage to debt, periodic attacks of panic when annual bills come due, guilt when you spend money, and arguments over money, a realistic budget frees you from financial pressure, worry, and arguments, provided, of course, that you plan your spending and spend according to your plan.

A BUDGET WORKSHEET

Monthly Income

Monthly income (twice a monthly x 2, bi-weekly x 2.167, weekly x 4.333) __________
Other income __________
Total *monthly* income __________

Monthly Expenses

Charitable giving __________
Savings __________
Home
- Mortgage payment (or rent) __________
- Taxes (yearly expense ÷ 12) __________
- Utilities (*monthly* water, electricity, & gas) __________
- Phone (home phone and cellular) __________
- Supscriptions, internet __________
- Homeowners Insurance __________
- Gardener, pool, etc. __________
- Other household expenses __________
- Food (including groceries, household items and fast food) __________

Clothing
- Clothes (including adults and children) __________
- Cleaning (including dry cleaning and laundromat) __________

Transportation
- Car payment __________
- Car insurance __________
- Car maintenance __________
- Gasoline __________

Personal Insurance
- Life insurance __________
- Health insurance __________
- Disability insurance __________
- Dental insurance __________

Medical costs not covered by insurance ____________
Children
Diapers ____________
Child care ____________
Tuition ____________
Activities ____________
Allowances, etc. ____________

Total Debt payments (not including house or car) ____________

Entertainment ____________
Vacation (yearly expense ÷ 12) ____________
Christmas (yearly expense ÷ 12) ____________
Personal gifts like birthday presents (yearly expense ÷ 12) ____________
Misc. (hair care, newspaper, pets, hobbies, fees, goof-off, etc.) ____________

Total monthly expenses ____________

Difference between Income and Expenses (+ or -)

____

Chapter 4

THE DITCH BESIDE THE ROAD

If you now have a savings account that you are religiously using and a realistic budget you are rigorously following, you are on your way to accumulating wealth. Let's continue down the road that successful money accumulators must travel.The road is tricky. The tricky part is credit. If you are to succeed in accumulating wealth in our economic environment, you must travel this road. It's virtually impossible to get anywhere without going down the road of credit. The problem is that there is a ditch beside this road, and if you land in the ditch, you'll not make it very far, or at least, as fast down the road of wealth accumulation. The ditch is debt. The tricky part of traveling this necessary route is properly using credit while staying out of the ditch of debt.

Moses allowed for lending money (Deuteronomy 23:20; 28:12) but did not permit borrowing (Deuteronomy 28:12). As Solomon explains, "The borrower *is* servant to the lender" (Proverbs 22:7).

Credit

One of the financial facts of life is credit. The average person, and even rich people to some degree, cannot function in modern society without credit. Unless you have a great deal of money, without credit, you cannot buy a car or a house. Even if you have a lot of money and even own a home and a car, there are things you cannot do (or at least cannot do without difficulty) unless you have credit. For example, it is difficult to rent a car without a credit card. As a comedian pointed out, it's getting so bad in some places that if you want to pay cash, you have to show your credit card as a reference. So you need credit.

Credit Cards Here are some helpful hints concerning credit cards. Carefully consider the cost of a credit card. Cards vary in annual cost and in annual interest rates. Needless to say, you need to shop for the lowest-cost card.

Keep a list of all your credit cards. In a safe place at home, you should have a list of all your credit cards. This list should include all the information you would need if your cards are lost or stolen, including your name as it appears on the card, your card number, the address, and phone number of the credit card company, etc.

Pay off every card every month. Credit cards usually have very high interest rates. 18% is not uncommon. One study concluded that various fees, balance calculation methods, and extended payment schedules could result in real interest rates exceeding 30%. Regardless of your interest rate, you should pay off your credit card balance each month. If your balance is so high that you cannot, do everything you can to reduce that debt as quickly as possible. You must be in charge of your charge cards, or your charge cards will be in charge of you.

Credit Reports If you have a credit card, you have a credit report. You need to check your credit report at various credit reporting agencies. Studies have revealed a high rate of inaccuracy in these reports. These investigations have found blunders on 40% of the files. People with the same name, misspelled names, wrong addresses, and a wrong digit in a Social Security number can cause data from someone else's file to be put into yours. Ex-mates can also cause problems.

Credit Damage Unfortunately, literally millions of people have damaged their credit. The damage may or may not be the person's fault. Credit damage comes in several different forms.

You can get mistakes removed. To correct errors, correspond in writing. Supply proof. If necessary, enlist the Better Business Bureau, a local consumer-protection agency, the State Attorney General, or an attorney. You must contact each agency individually. Clearing up mistakes in one agency's file does not clear up the errors in the others. Request a corrected version of your report and a list of those who have inquired about your report in the last six months. You are entitled to this information by federal law.

Late payments, non-payments, collections, bankruptcies, judgments, etc., result in negatives on your report. As one fellow said, "I won't say what our credit is like, but if they look us up in

Dun and Bradstreet, we're dun!" By law, negative information can stay on your record for seven years. Bankruptcies can stay on for ten years. (Note: The Federal Credit Reporting Act only says that such information can be "maintained for no longer than seven years." It does not say "must.") What does a person do who has a negative on his or her report? According to the law, if you are unable to clear up your report, you are entitled to a 100-word explanation to be put in your file. This will not solve the bad credit, but it is better than nothing.

There are companies that—for a fee—will "dispute" your negatives. There is no such thing as credit repair, but there is a legitimate dispute process that can get negative items removed from your credit report.

Debt

If you have debts, especially credit card debt, you are paying "interest" that, as you know, is the price for credit. The higher the debt, the higher the interest. Interest costs money, a lot of money. When you purchase anything on credit, you pay much more for it than you would have if you had paid cash for it.

If you buy an item for $100 and charge it to a credit card with a large balance, you will pay for that $100 item for a long time. If you leave it on the credit card for one year, you will end up paying 15-21% interest. That means you would have paid $120 for that $100 item. Twenty dollars may not seem like much, but by the time you pay interest on all you purchase with credit, it can add up to hundreds and thousands of dollars.

Suppose you have $2000 in credit card debt and are paying $50 per month on it. You will not pay it off in the next year. You will not even pay it down to under $1000. That means you will be paying interest on at least $1,000 for a year. If the interest rate on your card is 19.8%, you will pay $198 in interest on $1000 of credit card debt in one year. In other words, you will owe $1198 at the end of the year instead of $1000. If that $1198 is allowed to stand for another year, you will pay 19.8% on $1198 ($237.20), bringing your debt at the end of the second year to $1435.20.

You have to pay the government for the privilege of earning and spending money (income and sales taxes). Why pay someone else for the privilege to spend money if you don't have to do so? Money talks; it says "good-bye," especially when paying interest.

Obviously, if these debts were paid in full, or at least reduced, you would save money. If your debts were paid off or reduced, the money you are now paying on them would be money in your pocket every month. It would be like getting a raise. For those with large debts, that raise would be substantial! Furthermore, the money spent on debt could be invested, earning you money rather than costing you money. Debt is costly. You are losing the interest you are paying because of it, and the money you could be making if you had it invested. If you would like to eliminate, or at least reduce, your debt, see "My Action Plan" on debt reduction at the end of this chapter.

Summary: To manage your money effectively and assist in your overall goal of accumulating wealth, you should get and maintain good credit and avoid interest.

A clarification is in order. On the one hand, you need credit, which means you'll have to pay interest. On the other hand, you should avoid interest at all costs. What do you do? Proceed with caution. You need a credit card, and you need to establish credit. Interest is the price you pay for a credit rating. At the same time, as much as possible, avoid interest, especially high credit card interest. You can avoid paying interest on a credit card by paying it in full every month.

MY ACTION PLAN: REDUCING DEBT

Those deep in debt often think a consolidation loan will solve their problem. Assuming you can get one, a consolidation loan may very well reduce monthly debt *payments*; although it could save you some money on interest, it will not reduce the *total debt*. An extreme measure is bankruptcy, which, of course, has serious consequences, such as being on your credit report for ten years. Beyond those measures, there are three ways you can *reduce* your debt.

Step 1: Reduce the Amount of Debt

Obviously, the simplest way to reduce your debt is to reduce the amount of the debt. If you have extra money in your checking or savings account, consider applying some of it to your debt. Increase your income by working overtime or get a temporary part-time job. Cut expenses. Cut one to five percent on everything possible, from food to vacation. Sell something. Have a garage sale! Reducing the debt saves money on interest.

Another approach is debt negotiation. Either you or an organization that provides this service can negotiate with your creditors to reduce your debt.

Step 2: Reduce the Interest Rate

If you cannot reduce the amount of the debt, reduce the interest rate. Call each card issuer and request an interest rate reduction of at least 2%. Be persistent. Speak to several levels of supervisors. Change to cards with lower interest rates. The lower rate may be temporary. So, when the lower rate expires, switch to another card with a lower interest rate.

Step 3: Accelerate the Debt Payments

You can reduce your debt faster by accelerating your debt payments. First, list all your debts by the number of payments remaining. At the top of the list, put the debt with the fewest number of payments remaining. Continue the list until the one with the most payments due is last. Then, when the one with the fewest number of payments left is paid in full, add the amount of that payment to the second card on the list. Continue that procedure until all debts are paid. This process will accelerate your debt reduction.

This assumes that you are financially able to continue making the same total credit card payments you are now making on all your credit cards until all the cards are paid in full. Needless to say, if you also do not add any more charges, you will pay off your current credit card debt even faster.

Chapter 5

PROTECT YOURSELF ON THE ROAD

The road to accumulating wealth can be tricky and *dangerous*. The tricky part is the debt ditch. The danger is the possibility of loss. The loss of your car or house could wipe you out financially. Insurance protects you from that loss. The premature death of the breadwinner means the loss of income for those depending on the breadwinner. Life insurance protects from the loss of income. So you need to protect yourself and your obligations. In other words, you need insurance.

In some cases, you are required to have insurance. For example, virtually all states require car owners to have car insurance. A mortgage company may require that you have life insurance to cover indebtedness on your home. Beyond being required to have insurance, you need it because it is smart. You need insurance for protection. That's the whole concept behind insurance. Furthermore, insurance can also allow tax-deferred accumulation of money.

The word "insurance" comes from a French word for "sure"

and means "protection from loss." Insurance is nothing more than spreading the chance of financial loss among a large number of people. It began in the 13th century. Ship owners in England had the potential loss of their ships and/or their cargo. So groups of ship owners and wealthy individuals met at coffeehouses in London to pool money to cover any losses at sea. (In the 17th century, the leading coffeehouse became Lloyds of London.) Fire insurance was first offered in the 16th century. Benjamin Franklin began the first fire insurance company in the U.S. in 1752. It was named the Philadelphia Contribution-ship for the Insurance of Houses from Loss by Fire. Insurance is also a legal contract (that is, an agreement that the courts will enforce) in which, in exchange for the payment of premiums, an insurance company promises to pay a sum of money upon a loss. Perhaps, ultimately, the concept could be said to be rooted in the biblical statement, "Bear one another's burdens, and so fulfill the law of Christ" (Galatians 6:2).

Actually, life insurance today is not just about pooling money and taking losses out of the pool. Modern life insurance is based on the law of large numbers, which states that the larger the number of homogeneous units in one group, the more predictable the number of future losses of that group within a given period of time. In other words, insurance companies deal only with averages; they can only predict the average number of losses for a particular group. Furthermore, the larger the number, the more accurate the prediction. Given a large number of people the same age, gender, and with certain risk characteristics, such as whether or not the person smokes or is in a risky occupation, they can predict with reasonable accuracy the average number of deaths in that group per year. They then add these "mortality" charges (also called "the cost of insurance") and the administrative costs to arrive at the premium amount.

However insurance works, the point is you need insurance to protect your assets. Let us discuss car insurance, homeowners insurance, health insurance, disability insurance, and life insurance. Remember, the basic concept of insurance is protection from a possible loss. Therefore, in each area, you should ask, "What is the possible loss?" and "What protection do I need?"

Car Insurance

As I pointed out in the introduction, I have never had a property and causality license. That is, I have not had a license to sell car insurance or homeowners' insurance. My intention here is to offer a brief introduction to the concept. It is *not* to give an exhaustive discussion of these types of insurance.

The Possible Losses Remember that the basic concept of insurance is that it is a contract to protect you against financial loss. When you own a car, you have several possibilities of loss.

1. There is the possibility that your car will hit someone or something, causing "bodily injury" or "property damage," for which you will be liable.

2. There is the possibility that your car will be damaged in

a collision.

3. There is the possibility that your car will be stolen or damaged in some way other than in an accident, like in a fire.

4. There is the possibility that you could be injured in an accident.

5. There is the possibility that your car will break down and will need to be towed.

6. There is the possibility that after an accident, you may need to rent a car while your car is being repaired.

7. There is the possibility of a loss of "special equipment."

8. There is the possibility that an uninsured motorist will hit your car.

Automobile insurance has been created to cover each of these possibilities. The question is, how much of this "coverage" do you need?

The Protection You Need Look at each possible loss and determine the protection you need in each category.

1. Liability insurance. If your car caused bodily injury or property damage, it could cost you everything you have. Liability insurance protects you against these types of losses. Virtually all states require a car owner to have liability insurance to register and operate a car.

2. Collision and comprehension coverage. This type of insurance covers your car. The amount of collision and comprehensive coverage depends on the car's value and the deductible.

3. Other kinds of car insurance. The other possible losses

covered by car insurance are bodily injury, the possibility that your car will break down and need to be towed, or that you will need a rental car after an accident.

With these possible losses and the protection needed to cover them in mind, you should sit down with a professional in this area and determine exactly the car insurance you need.

Homeowners Insurance

Homeowners should consider homeowners' insurance. The following description covers only the basics. Much, much more could be said.

The Possible Losses To determine how much homeowners' insurance you need, begin by looking at the possible losses.

1. First, there is the possibility that your house could be partially or completely destroyed and you could be forced to live somewhere else for months and rebuild.

2. There is also the possibility that you could lose the furnishings inside the house.

3. Beyond those losses are others, such as someone getting hurt on your property, loss of personal possessions, etc.

The Protection You Need The basic homeowner policy is called HO1. It covers damage from wind, fire, rain, lightning, explosions, and riots. HO2 and HO3 have broader coverage. The first question you should ask in this area is, "Do you need to cover the cost to rebuild your house if it were destroyed?" You can save some money on your homeowner's insurance by choosing a higher deductible.

You should also consider obtaining coverage for loss of furnishings and for the possibility that someone will be injured on your property.

The coverage you get beyond these possible losses depends on you and your location. For example, if you have personal valuables such as silver, jewelry, or furs, you can buy a separate policy called a "floater."

Again, with these possible losses and the protection needed to cover them in mind, you should sit down with a professional in this area and determine precisely the homeowner's policy you need.

Health and Disability Insurance

The next area of insurance you need to consider is health and disability. Many have health insurance at work. Most do not have disability insurance. With more and more people either not having these benefits at work or being self-employed, it is helpful to at least touch on some rudiments of these types of insurance.

The Possible Losses The possible losses are obvious. You can get sick and require hospitalization, or you can be temporarily or permanently disabled and unable to work.

The Protection You Need Many people have health insurance through their work. If that is the case and you pay part of the premium, you should check into the possibility of buying coverage for your family outside the coverage that you can obtain through your employer. It may be cheaper. A bank employee got cheaper insurance for his children by buying it outside the bank. Of course, that might not be so in your case. Check this out carefully.

Health insurance will help with your medical bills, but if you are unable to work, you may not have an income. To cover that possible loss, you need disability insurance. This is a greater possibility than most think. According to the Social Security Administration, about one in four (25%) of today's 20-year-olds will experience a disability lasting 90 days or more before they reach retirement age.

There are three issues concerning DI (disability insurance): 1) an elimination period, that is, the number of days before the insurance pays, either 30, 60, 90, 180, or 365 days. The longer the elimination period, the *lower the policy cost*. If you have enough savings to cover your expenses for three months, consider a policy with a 90-day waiting period rather than a 30-day one. 2) The benefit period, the period during which the policy pays (either 24 months, 30 months, 5 years, to age 65, or for a lifetime). The longer the period, the *more* expensive the insurance. Many suggest buying coverage that pays only to age 65, rather than for life, because you can collect Social Security at 65. 3) The benefit amount, which is determined by your current occupation, will be either 50% or 60% of your annual salary.

DI either covers being unable to work at your own occupation or at any occupation. Your "own occupation" pays if you are unable to work at your occupation, even if you could work at another occupation. An "any occupation" policy defines disability as the inability to work in any occupation.

Life Insurance

The last area of insurance we need to look at is life insurance. Again, the issue is: what losses could life insurance cover? This list might surprise you.

The Possible Losses As with other types of insurance, there are possible losses that can be covered by life insurance.

1. If the breadwinner or a spouse contributing financially to the family were to die, there would be a loss of family income. There are also other costs connected with dying. Obviously, there will be funeral expenses. There can be doctor and hospital bills from an illness or accident, but the big issue is the loss of income for your family.

2. If you have a mortgage or other debts and you were to die, there would be a loss of your income to pay off debts.

3. If you have minor children who want to go to college, your death could mean the loss of the cost of their college education.

4. People who have worked for many years for a company that has a pension plan can "lose" part of their pension, that is, not get the maximum, by selecting the wrong option.

5. Retired people without a company pension suffer a substantial "loss" of income when they retire because they do not have a pension.

6. The estate of some suffers a "loss" in the sense that the

survivors have to pay estate taxes.

7. Children and grandchildren can sustain the "loss of an inheritance" because there is nothing to inherit.

The Protection You Need Life insurance can protect against all the losses listed above, but it is not as simple as buying a policy to cover them. The reason is that there are different types of life insurance. So first, you should answer the question of how much insurance is needed, and then, you should determine which kind of life insurance is best in your situation.

Generally, several of the losses listed above are lumped together. Family income and related issues are considered the first and foremost needs for life insurance. How much insurance is needed to cover the loss of family income and other losses related to the death of the breadwinner? The standard answer to that question is: first, determine how much money those who are dependent on you will need if you should die. That amount includes final illness expenses, funeral expenses, possible taxes, mortgage payments, debts, living expenses, educational costs, and other future expenses. Then, subtract from that figure whatever resources they will have. Ideally, you should have enough life insurance to come as close as you can afford to make up the difference between what your dependents would need if you were to die and what they would have. In other words, final expenses + dependents' needs (consider their resources) × their years to retirement = your insurance need. This method has been shortened and summarized with the expression, "To determine your life insurance need, use a DIME," meaning death (expenses), income (to be replaced), mortgage, and education.

A career insurance salesman who has been in the business for years once told me that even though his company has a worksheet for people to use to determine how much life insurance they need, he never uses it. He said that after dealing with about a thousand clients, he had never failed to see one that, after accounting for Social Security and inflation, didn't need from eight to ten times their annual salary. That rule of thumb is not bad.

Beyond the general family income protection need, the amount of life insurance a person needs is determined by the potential loss being covered. For example, if the mortgage or another debt is the only issue, the amount of insurance needed is determined by the amount of the debt (or mortgage). A man who borrowed $25,000 for five years from his sister purchased a life insurance policy to cover that debt if he should die. If college education is the concern, the cost of that education can be covered if you were to die.

The possible loss of part of a pension can also be covered with life insurance. For example, an employee at retirement could be given one of three options: 1) $2000.00 a month as long as he lives, but nothing is paid to his spouse upon his death. 2) $1600.00 a month for as long as either he or his wife is alive. 3) $1800 a month as long as he lives, and upon his death, his wife would receive $900.00 a month for the rest of her life. Under such circumstances, most choose option two to protect their wives, yet lose $400.00 per month of retirement income.

Life insurance can be used to replace the employee's income for the surviving spouse, thereby allowing the employee to choose option one at retirement.

Life insurance has been used to cover other specific financial losses, such as estate taxes and money intended as an inheritance for children or grandchildren.

As we shall see shortly, some types of life insurance build up cash value that can be withdrawn or borrowed. This has been called the "living benefit" of life insurance. Some have taken out insurance to provide for their children's college education. In such cases, they use the policy's cash value to meet this need. Social Security alone, or in many cases Social Security and a company pension, will not provide a comfortable retirement. So, some have used the cash value of their insurance to supplement their retirement income.

Why would anyone use life insurance to finance the college education of his or her children or for retirement income? Why not just invest the money in some other instrument? Why life insurance? The answer is that life insurance has always enjoyed a favorable tax status. For example, a beneficiary does not have to pay income tax on the death benefit received from a life insurance policy. There are other tax advantages to life insurance. In some cases, the cash accumulation from an insurance policy can be borrowed interest-free, and as long as the policy stays in effect, no taxes need to be paid! These features offer the possibility of college funding and/or retirement. In these cases, life insurance is used not only for the death benefit to protect against a loss, but also for the living benefit of a tax-deferred cash reserve that can, under certain circumstances, be withdrawn tax-free.

Having decided on the amount of life insurance you need, the next issue is to determine the type of life insurance you should obtain. There are two basic types of life insurance: Term and Permanent. The first life insurance policy on record was issued in 1563. For the next 200 years, all life policies were short-term (or endowment policies, meaning the face amount is paid to the insured if he or she lives to the end of the policy period).

1. Term Life Insurance. Term insurance is pure insurance, simply providing a death benefit. It covers the insured for a specific number of years. For that reason, it is called temporary insurance, meaning it is not intended to last throughout the insured's expected life span. The term can be for any number of years. The most common terms are one-year, five-year, ten-year, 15-year, and 20-year. Permanent insurance is designed to last until one dies.

The different types of term policies are defined by how the face amount, that is, the amount listed on the face page (the first page) of the policy (in other words, the death benefit), changes throughout the life of the policy. The face amount may increase, stay level, or decrease.

With *increasing term*, the death benefit increases periodically.

The second kind of term life insurance is *level term*. It has a level death benefit, usually with level premiums: the coverage and the premium remain level for the specified period stated in the policy, usually five to twenty years. All insurance is based on the insured's age, sex, and risk characteristics. Therefore, premiums increase over time because the insurance company assumes that the older a person gets, the greater the risk of death. (As life expectancy decreases, yearly premiums increase.) To arrive at a level premium, the insurance company adds up the cost for the total term, say five or ten years, and divides by the number of years to arrive at an average payment. They also account for the fact that they receive extra premium income in the early years, which can reduce the overall cost. Note, however, this level, average premium may not be guaranteed for the full term. (The premiums of a level term policy, that is, one with a level death benefit, may also increase while the death benefit remains the same. Annual or yearly renewable term has a fixed death benefit for a premium that increases each year.)

The third type of term insurance is decreasing term insurance. The premium remains the same, but the coverage decreases annually. The policy ends when the insurance amount reaches zero. This type has been used as mortgage insurance. Because few decreasing term policies are based on current mortality and interest assumptions, they are not considered cost-effective.

Term life insurance can be either renewable or reentry. Reentry or a non-guaranteed term expires at the end of the term, and the policyholder has to reapply to continue coverage, which means taking another physical. If there is a new health problem, the insurance company can either decline the application or change the risk category, thereby charging a higher rate. Annual renewable term guarantees that the policy can be renewed without evidence of insurability (no medical exam is needed) as long as the premiums are paid. In return for this guarantee, a higher premium is charged.

Term insurance is either convertible or it is not. A convertible term gives the insured the right to switch to permanent insurance at some point in the future. Of course, there is an additional charge for this feature.

When is it appropriate to buy term? The answer is 1) when a person needs insurance for a short time or 2) when a person wants to supplement other types of insurance. Which type of term should you purchase? An annual renewable term is suited for individuals who need insurance for a relatively short time, such as 1 to 4 years. The rates for annual renewable term are usually guaranteed for only three years or less. Over longer periods, a level term is more cost-effective than an annual renewable term. Therefore, it is suited for individuals who need coverage for 5 to 10 years. Beyond ten years, some argue that level term is the best buy and even that term insurance is the only kind anyone should ever buy, but that is a hotly debated issue. Others argue that some forms of permanent insurance are a better choice for periods of more than 10 years.

2. Whole Life Insurance. In 1762, the Society for the Equitable Assurance of Lives and Survivorships (one of Britain's leading life insurance companies, today known as "Old Equitable") introduced a level-premium, fixed-sum, whole-life policy. Hence, whole life, the first form of permanent insurance, was born. As its name implies, it is designed to cover

the whole of life, usually assumed to be 100 years. Remember, all life insurance is based on the insured's age at the time the policy is written (as well as gender and risk characteristics), and the cost of insurance increases as the insured gets older. Whole life assumes the insured will live 100 years and averages the cost. Thus, the premiums are "level," that is, they remain the same every year. In fact, in a traditional whole life policy, the premium amount cannot increase at any time for any reason.

Whole life and, for that matter, all forms of permanent life insurance consist of a death benefit plus an accumulation of cash value. Because premiums are averaged, the policyholder of a whole life policy ends up paying more at the beginning than the insurance cost. The "extra" money, that is, the money above the cost of insurance for that year, is called "cash value." This cash value accumulates over the years, and it earns interest. Whole life, then, is insurance and "forced savings" combined. The cash value grows tax-deferred and can be used to pay premiums, buy more insurance, be borrowed, or withdrawn. If the insured lives to the assumed age without using the cash build-up, the policy will pay the face amount.

There are two basic types of whole life: traditional and interest-sensitive. Traditional whole life guarantees both the death benefit and the interest rate. An interest-sensitive whole life policy guarantees the death benefit but pays only the current interest rate on the cash value. Thus, interest-sensitive whole life does not have the guarantee that traditional whole life does.

Whole life is appropriate for those who want permanent

insurance, meaning all of their lives, but do not want to pay higher premiums of term insurance or any premiums when they get older.

The problem with whole life is that the interest rate on the cash value accumulating is usually lower than current rates. Some object that whole life is a "bad" investment. They say "buy term and invest the difference," meaning, if you bought term and invested the difference between the term premium and what the whole life premium would have been, you would make more than the insurance company would pay you.

There is some truth to that objection, but it also raises several problems. For one thing, it looks good on paper, but in reality, it simply does not work for the vast majority of people, because they outlive their term, choose to cancel (lapse) the policy when their financial needs change, or stop paying their premiums. So problem number one with "buying term and investing the difference" is that people in the real world don't keep buying the term! Furthermore, many (probably most) don't invest the difference! Besides, the life insurance industry has created other types of permanent insurance that can give you a greater return on the cash value. Those two types are called universal life and variable universal life. There are other problems. For example, this approach assumes that no one needs life insurance as they get older, which may not be true.

3. Universal Life Insurance. During the 1970s, interest rates soared. Savers began putting their money into either treasury bills or money market funds. In 1979, the Federal Trade Commission released the results of a multi-year study showing that returns

on whole life policies held for 20 years averaged only 2-4.5%. Policies held for shorter periods actually earned negative rates. Policyholders responded by borrowing the cash value at 4.5% or 5% and reinvesting the proceeds in money market funds earning 10% or more. All of this persuaded the insurance companies to offer a better deal. Hence, universal life insurance was created.

Universal life, like whole life, is a form of permanent insurance, but unlike whole life, which is usually not flexible, universal life is very flexible. The premiums can be changed as long as sufficient payments are made to keep the policy in force. The death benefit can be increased or decreased as needed, subject to insurability requirements. The interest rates and minimum guaranteed rates are higher. It is important to note that in a universal life policy, the insurance company determines the return by setting an interest rate that it can change periodically.

There are other features of a universal life contract that make it attractive. The cash value grows tax-deferred, and some companies allow the policyholder, under certain circumstances, to borrow the accumulated cash value at no interest. On top of all that, the loan does not have to be repaid as long as the policy is in force (it will be deducted from the death benefit).

4. Variable Universal Life. Variable universal life is also a form of permanent life insurance. Like universal life, it is flexible. The main difference between universal life and variable universal life is that, with variable universal life, the cash value is placed in a separate account and invested in mutual fund sub-accounts. Thus, the insured, not the insurance company, has

control over the return. It should be pointed out, however, that while the return in a variable policy can be greater than the return in a universal contract, the variable return could also be less. It is possible that, at some point, the policyholder might have to pay more into the policy just to keep the insurance portion in force. So with the possibility of greater return comes greater risk.

Because of the complexities of life insurance, most people need a professional to advise them.

An agent asked a potential client, "If you had a machine that made money, would you insure it?" The most reasonable answer, of course, is "Yes." Well, the breadwinner(s) of a family is the money-making machine, so to speak. The logical thing to do is to ensure that at least some of the money comes in if something happens to the "machine."

To say the same thing another way, as some agents have asked, "If you owned a goose that laid golden eggs, would you insure the goose or would you insure the golden eggs?" You might insure the eggs, but you would for sure insure the goose! Likewise, the breadwinner of a family provides the income for the "golden eggs" of a house and a car. Without hesitation, some insure the house and the car but hesitate to purchase life insurance on the breadwinner. Buying homeowners' and car insurance but not life insurance is like insuring the eggs and not the goose.

Summary: To help you accumulate wealth, you need enough insurance to cover the possibilities of your car being damaged, your home being destroyed, your health being disabled, and your life ending in death, with the result being financial ruin.

If the object is to accumulate wealth, why spend money on insurance, especially life insurance? Isn't that a waste of money? In some cases, it can be. If the wrong type of life insurance is used, it could end up costing more than necessary. On the other hand, insurance can help provide the wealth you are trying to accumulate to reach your goals in a way like no other. For example, if you began a $100-per-month savings program and died a month later, your family would have $100. If, however, you purchased $100,000 worth of insurance with that $100 and died the first month, then your family would have $100,000. As an article in the *Wall Street Journal* once said, "A sound financial plan begins with insurance."

The *Talmud* contains the story of a man who sold one-kilogram bags of wheat. When the inspectors checked his bags, they discovered that there were only 900 grams of wheat and 100 grams of a preservative. The question was, "Was the merchant cheating his customers?" Most would conclude that the vendor did not cheat his customers because, without the preservative, all of the wheat would be ruined. Insurance is like the preservative in the bag of wheat. It is using a portion of your resources to protect the rest.

MY ACTION PLAN: DETERMINING MY LIFE INSURANCE NEEDS

Just exactly how much life insurance do *you* need? There are several different ways to determine that. Perhaps, in the final analysis, there is no one right answer. Maybe it is better to suggest that each person has a correct range. Use the following three methods to get three perspectives on a range for your needs.

Step 1: Use the Simplest Suggestion

The simplest approach is to use the rule of thumb that says a person should have five to seven, or maybe even ten, times their annual salary in life insurance.

Annual salary __________ times 5 equals ___________
Annual salary __________ times 7 equals ___________
Annual salary __________ times 10 equals __________

Step 2: Use a Moderate Method

A moderate method suggests choosing the amount by multiplying your annual salary by a number based on your lifestyle.

Low mortgage, no children at home 3 to 5 x salary
and surviving spouse is willing to work ______________

Moderate mortgage, money in savings
5 to 7 x salary = and surviving spouse
is willing to work ______________

Expensive mortgage, young children and
7 to 9 x salary = surviving spouse wants
choice of not working ______________

Step 3: Use a Formal Formula

A more formal procedure is to figure out exactly what is needed.

Funeral expenses ________________
Mortgage debt ________________
Living expenses of dependents ________________
Future educational needs ________________
Total ________________

Minus available resources (including existing
insurance) ________________

Additional insurance needed ________________

Chapter 6

THE HOUSE BESIDE THE ROAD

Beside the road on the way to wealth accumulation should be a house you call home. Homeownership is a major part of the American dream. Everyone wants to own a house with no mortgage. For many, it is a matter of security. From a strictly financial point of view, homeownership is a good idea for several reasons.

First, money spent on rent has no return, whereas money spent on a mortgage builds equity. In popular parlance, paying rent is like throwing money down a rat hole. When, however, you are paying off a mortgage, you are buying something that *can* make you money (of course, you may also lose money!). Moreover, in an overall financial plan, real estate is part of the diversification strategy.

Second, mortgage interest is currently tax-deductible, saving homeowners money on their taxes. Furthermore, the property taxes are also deductible. So, solely from a financial point of view, homeownership is part of managing money and accumulating wealth.

Assuming that you are either going to purchase your first

home or that in the future you will buy another one, there are several financial issues you need to consider before you sign on the dotted line. Like other topics we've covered, this discussion is not intended to be exhaustive. The material will start with the most basic issues and advance from there. Here, then, are items to consider when purchasing a house.

Price Range

Obviously, the first financial issue is, "What can I afford?" meaning, for what size loan can I qualify? How do mortgage-lending institutions determine if a person qualifies for a loan?

The Industry Standard The *standard* for a conventional loan is set by the secondary market, not the lending institution. The Federal National Mortgage Association is a private company that buys mortgages from leading companies. This secondary market sets the standard. The lender sets the loan's interest rate.

When lenders review your loan applications, they consider factors such as income, assets, credit, and liabilities to determine whether a loan qualifies for the secondary market. Here are some of the specifics.

- Having a steady income enables you to repay the loan. The issue is "steady employment," defined as working continuously for 2 years or more. Having the same job is not the issue; the issue is that the job change resulted in equal or higher pay and continued use of proven skills. There are acceptable reasons for not having worked continuously for 2 years, such as a military discharge.

- The down payments cannot be unverified or borrowed from undocumented sources. Secondary market guidelines require a clear, documented paper trail for all funds used in a transaction.
- Being able to make monthly payments is critical. To determine your ability to make monthly mortgage payments, they look at two commonly accepted *guidelines*: a) your monthly housing cost (P. I. T. I., that is, the principal, interest, taxes, and insurance) and b) your total monthly debt (including house payments, car loans, installment debt).
- Having paid past bills on time indicates you will pay in the future. So you need good credit. (Wait 7 years after a foreclosure and 2 years after a Chapter 13 bankruptcy, and 4 years after a Chapter 7 bankruptcy.)

One reason to save money regularly is to have the money for a down payment on a house.

Variations As you probably know, people qualify for loans without meeting those standards. There are variations. Also, some of the specifics change from time to time. So check the current specifics.

Location

The foremost maxim of buying a house is "location, location, location." The house you want may be closer to work or grandma, but from a financial point of view, the three most important issues are location, location, location because the location will determine the price. Just exactly what does the expression "location, location, location" mean?

The Town For the maximum resale price, you need to buy a house in the right town. Large cities in America are made up not just of one city but a major city surrounded by suburbs and towns. Any native knows which town is the most desirable and what area is—shall we say, is "the least desirable." The most basic economic fact of real estate life is that the most desirable is the most expensive. The assumption is that if it is the most desirable and, therefore, the most expensive now, it will be that way later when you sell your house. This most desirable town is determined by 1) natural advantage: next to water, on top of a hill, etc., 2) economic advantage—the most expensive homes are built there, and 3) education advantage—the best schools are there.

When I moved to Dallas in the mid-1970s, the most desirable area was Highland Park, followed by North Dallas, Richardson, Garland, and so on. For middle-income families, the most desirable, affordable option was Richardson, followed by Garland. When buying a house, get in the most "expensive" town you can afford.

The Section of Town For the maximum resale value, you need to buy a house in the right section of the right town. Every town or suburb has different sections or "neighborhoods." Some sections are considered the "best." These various sections of a town are marked off by something. We speak of "being from the other side of the tracks" because years ago, and, in some places to this day, the railroad tracks were the dividing line between the desirable and the undesirable parts of town. A street is often the line of demarcation. In Glendora, CA, prices go up the higher you go in the foothills. Streets mark off the various price ranges. The residents speak of "above Foothill" (a street), "above Sierra Madre" (another street), and "above Palm" (name of another street). In some cities, the freeway has replaced the railroad tracks. The issue is living north or south, or east or west, of the freeway.

This is even true within mobile home parks. I visited a mobile home park that was divided into two parts. The back of the park was slightly higher than the front. The height difference was about a foot. Yet, the residents of the back, higher part of the park, referred to the lower end as "the ghetto."

In Southern California, San Marino is known for being wealthy, exclusive, and very expensive. Yet, the natives know that within San Marino, there are different areas. The locals will tell you that there is Super Marino, San Marino, and Sub Marino. When buying a home, get into the most expensive section of town you can afford.

The Street In the discussion of location, location, location, we have come to the street itself. The rule here is don't buy the most expensive house on the block. It will not appreciate as well as the others. Do buy a house with "curb appeal" and, if at all possible, buy at least a three-bedroom house because it will have better resale value.

Since we are down to the house itself, unless you don't have a choice, do not buy a condo or a mobile home. (The exception is planning to stay in it for the rest of your life.) Condos and mobile homes have fees that can be expensive and they do not have good resale value. They do not appreciate as much as houses, and they do not sell as fast. As a financial planner once said to me, "You want to own the dirt."

Right, you want to own the best dirt, which means owning dirt on the most desirable street, in the most desirable neighborhood, in the most desirable town. Don't buy the most expensive house on the block; buy a less expensive house in the most expensive neighborhood you can afford. Remember, it's location, location, location because the most desirable will appreciate better. It's the law of supply and demand. Buy what others will want when you are ready to sell.

The Loan

Another consideration is the loan. You need to understand the types and lengths of loans, as well as some creative ideas about loans.

Types of Loans The two *basic* types of loans are fixed and variable. A fixed loan has a guaranteed fixed interest rate throughout the life of the loan. A variable loan has an interest rate that can (and does) change. It begins below the fixed rate and can go above it. There are also combinations of these. For example, there are loans with a three-, five-, or ten-year variable rate that then roll over to a fixed rate.

Which type should you get? There are several factors to consider. You may only qualify for a variable. Some insist on a fixed-interest-rate loan because they do not like the payment fluctuations that can and do occur with a variable-rate loan. Frankly, the possibilities are so many, and the factors are so complicated that you should talk to a professional before you decide which type of loan to get.

The Length of the Loan The length of a home loan can be any number of years, from three to forty years. The two most common are 30-year and 15-year loans. Which one should you get?

Some argue that you should get a 15-year loan. The monthly payments will be higher, but your house will be paid off in 15 years, saving you thousands of dollars in interest. For some people, like a 50-year-old man who wants to have his house paid for by age 65, that may be a good idea.

For others, it may not be the best financial decision. For one thing, if you have a 30-year loan instead of a 15-year loan, you will save more on taxes. Remember, mortgage interest is one of the last big deductions middle-income Americans have. On top of that, you may be able to make money with a 30-year mortgage as compared to a 15-year mortgage. A 30-year mortgage costs less per month than a 15-year mortgage. If you invested the difference between the two and made an average rate of return, you could conceivably have enough in 15 years to pay off the mortgage and then some. So consider taking a 30-year loan, financing the difference.

Summary: To accumulate wealth and reduce your taxes, you should purchase a home in the most desirable location possible with a fixed rate.

MY ACTION PLAN: CALCULATING A MORTGAGE PAYMENT

Step 1: Match the Interest Rate and the Years of the Loan

To determine the monthly payments, begin by matching the interest rate and the loan term. Example: a 6% 30-year loan equals $6.00 per $ 1,000. For a 3% loan, divide it in half. Whatever the percent, do the math.

Step 2: Multiply the Results by the Number of 1000's of the Loan

Example: for a $250,000 loan: 6.00 × 250 = $ 1,500; that is, $1,500 is the monthly payment for a $250,000 loan for 30 years at 6%. This is only principal and interest. It does not include taxes and insurance. For a $500,00 loan, double it, etc.

Now figure your mortgage payment.

Interest rate x number of years ________________

Multiply by the number of 1000's of the loan amount

____

Total is the principal and interest payment only

____

MONTHLY PAYMENTS PER $1,000

Interest	15 Years	20 Years	30 Years
4.50%	$7.65	$6.33	$5.07
4.75%	$7.78	$6.46	$5.22
5.00%	$7.91	$6.60	$5.37
5.25%	$8.04	$6.74	$5.52
5.50%	$8.17	$6.88	$5.68
5.75%	$8.30	$7.02	$5.84
6.00%	$8.44	$7.16	$6.00
6.25%	$8.57	$7.31	$6.16
6.50%	$8.71	$7.46	$6.32
6.75%	$8.85	$7.60	$6.49
7.00%	$8.99	$7.75	$6.65
7.25%	$9.13	$7.90	$6.82
7.50%	$9.27	$8.06	$6.99
7.75%	$9.41	$8.21	$7.16
8.00%	$9.56	$8.36	$7.34
8.25%	$9.70	$8.52	$7.51
8.50%	$9.85	$8.68	$7.69
8.75%	$9.99	$8.84	$7.87
9.00%	$10.14	$9.00	$8.05

Chapter 7

AVOIDING THE TOLL ROAD

On your financial journey, you will encounter toll roads (taxes). Taxes are necessary and should be paid. When Jesus was asked, "Is it lawful to pay taxes to Caesar, or not?" (Matthew. 22:17), He said, "Render therefore to Caesar the things that are Caesar's, and to God the things that are God's" (Matthew. 22:21). Paul said something similar: "Render therefore to all their due: taxes to whom taxes *are due,* customs to whom customs, fear to whom fear, honor to whom honor" (Romans 13:7). All necessary taxes should be paid, but if it is legally possible to avoid some taxes, it will save you money.

When this country was founded, there was no income tax. The first comprehensive individual income tax was not enacted until 1862. It lasted only 10 years and had a top rate of 10%. In 1895, the Supreme Court ruled that taxes on personal income were unconstitutional. In 1913, the 16th Amendment was added to the Constitution. It says, "Congress shall have the power to lay and collect taxes on income from whatever source desired."

Since then, income taxes have become a hard fact of economic life in the United States.

In 1976, the IRS published a handbook for IRS agents. It stated, "During a state of national emergency resulting from enemy attack, the essential functions of the Service will be as follows: 1) assessing, collecting, and recording taxes." The government is going to collect taxes no matter what, even during a national emergency, even if you die (estate taxes)!

Everyone has to pay taxes, but the tax code itself allows for exemptions, commonly called loopholes. These provisions allow you to avoid, reduce, and defer taxes legally. You can save money that will enable you to accumulate wealth faster by taking advantage of what the tax code allows you to do. You need to know the options now and stay current every year you file. *Currently, these are some of the things you need to know, but tax laws constantly change. So, you should consult an accountant.*

Before looking at ways to reduce our tax liability, consider the number of taxes we pay.

- *Federal income taxes.* For starters, we pay federal income tax. In the past, the highest bracket has reached 70%. If you don't understand why Uncle Sam wears such a tall hat, you will when he passes it around.
- *State income taxes.* Many, but not all, states have an income tax in addition to the federal income tax.
- *Sales tax.* Then there is sales tax.
- *Excise tax.* An excise tax is a tax or duty on the

manufacture, sale, or consumption of various commodities within a country, such as tobacco, liquor, etc.

- *Gas tax.* If you drive a car, you pay taxes on every gallon of gas you buy.
- *Property tax.* If you own real estate (a house, etc.), you pay property tax.
- There are other taxes, such as gift and estate taxes.

It's amazing how many taxes there are. I've heard that what we need is a government handout, that is, the government should take its hand out of our pockets.

The Tax Foundation, a Washington-based nonprofit research group, says that in 2006, everything you earned from January 1 to April 26 went toward taxes. According to the Tax Foundation, April 26th is "Tax Freedom Day." (In 2019, Tax Freedom Day was April 16th; see https://taxfoundation.org/?s=tax+freedom for the latest date.)

Taxes cost us so much; they have a significant impact on our ability to save money. Imagine how much money you would have in the bank if you had half of the taxes you have paid in your lifetime. Taxes can and should be legitimately cut.

As I have mentioned, I am not an accountant. You should consult a tax professional for ways to avoid, reduce, and defer taxes. Here is a brief description of these categories.

Ways to Avoid Taxes

Believe it or not, there are legal ways to avoid income taxes altogether. According to the IRS code, there is even something called tax-free!

Tax-Free Tax-free income is money received that is not reported. If you rent your primary residence or your vacation home for less than 14 days a year, the rental income is completely tax-free. You don't even have to report it on your tax return. A boat can qualify as a second residence if it has sleeping space, a toilet, and cooking facilities [IRC Section 280A(g)].

Tax-Exempt Tax-exempt means the amount is reported but not taxed. Municipal bond interest is tax-exempt. The problem with this approach is that you may be better off investing in something else and paying taxes on it, but if you want to avoid taxes, municipal bonds will do the trick. People in higher tax brackets often invest in municipal bonds to avoid taxes.

Ways to Reduce Taxes

If you can't avoid taxes, reduce them as much as possible. This can be done through tax deductions, tax credits, and tax shelters.

Tax Deductions A tax deduction is something that can be deducted from your income *before* you figure out how much tax you owe. Schedule A is the form for *personal* tax deductions. The first deduction listed on it is medical and dental expenses. The only such expenses that are deductible must be above a certain percentage of your adjusted income. So keep records of all medical expenses you pay, including health insurance premiums, doctor bills not paid by insurance, hospital bills not covered by insurance, dentist bills, glasses, hearing aids, drugs, and mileage to and from the doctor's office.

The next listed deduction is taxes. The deductible taxes are state and local income taxes and real estate taxes. The largest deduction will probably be the interest paid on your home mortgage. Other interest is not deductible. Charity gifts are deductible. Cash gifts to a church or an approved charity are deductible, and so are gifts of household goods and clothing. I have donated cars, furniture, and clothes to charitable causes, which allowed me to deduct hundreds of dollars. Mileage in connection with work done for a charity is also deductible. There are other personal deductions. Some can be large. Most are smaller, but these smaller ones add up quickly. These include 1) casualty and theft losses, 2) moving expenses, 3) some job expenses, 4) etc. All personal deductions have rules, regulations, limitations, etc. If you prepare your own tax forms, read the IRS explanations concerning these deductions before you take them.

The other thing you can do to take deductions is start a business. Schedule C is the form for business deductions. Business expenses are deductible, including interest paid on a business loan, business use of your home, business use of your car, business use of your computer, subscriptions for business-related publications, etc.

Contributions to a qualified retirement plan, such as an IRA, are deductible in the year they are made.

Tax Credits A tax credit is something that can be deducted from your income *after* you figure out how much tax you owe.

Tax credits are different from tax deductions. A tax deduction reduces taxable income; a tax credit is a direct, dollar-for-dollar reduction of taxes due. For example, someone in the 28% tax bracket who has a $1.00 *deduction* reduces their tax by 28 cents, but a $1.00 *tax credit* reduces taxes by $1.00. Tax credits are given to taxpayers who invest in special government-approved programs for affordable housing or historic buildings. For more details, see an accountant or stockbroker.

Tax Shelters A "tax shelter" is the deduction of passive losses. Before the Tax Reform Act of 1986, a taxpayer could invest in certain limited partnerships and write off any losses from those investments against other income, such as salary. Since the Tax Reform Act, investment losses can only be deducted from investment gains.

There is one exception. One tax shelter that still allows you to deduct large losses against ordinary income is oil and gas drilling. The problem is that there is a potential liability risk, which can be either temporary or permanent. In other words, if the investment has an underinsured casualty, such as a fire, another unexpected liability, or a lawsuit, the investor's personal assets, including their home, car, and bank accounts, can be attached by creditors.

There is also something called "tax-sheltered" annuities, but these are not a "tax shelter" in the strict sense of the term. They are only available to individuals who work for educational institutions, hospitals, or non-profit organizations. Within limits, contributions to a "tax-sheltered" annuity are deductible from taxes the year they are made and the money in an annuity grows tax-deferred. Thus, technically, they are tax-deductible and offer tax deferral, but they are not a "tax shelter."

Ways to Defer Taxes

If you can't avoid or reduce your taxes, defer them, meaning you pay them later when you are retired and are in a lower tax bracket. There are several ways to defer taxes.

Tax-Deferred One way to defer taxes is to put money into an insurance product, either an insurance policy or an annuity. The cash value in insurance policies grows tax-deferred. Annuities will be discussed in the chapter on investments.

Another way to defer taxes is with a retirement plan. Money put into a retirement plan, such as an IRA or a 401(k), grows tax-deferred. Some rules and restrictions must be followed, but again, the point is that the taxes on money put into a retirement plan are not paid now; they are paid during retirement, when your tax bracket will probably be lower.

When you put money into anything that is tax-deferred, you are not paying taxes, so you have more to invest. Consequently, your money multiples faster. The higher your tax bracket, the more important this factor becomes.

Other Options There are other options for deferring taxes. Not all of them are always available for everyone every year, but it's good to know about these possibilities so you can take advantage of them if you qualify. These include 1) arrange to be paid in a future year or years, 2) sell property on the installment plan so that the gains are spread over a number of years, and 3) take a retirement plan distribution in the form of an annuity spread over time rather than in a lump sum.

Summary: Taxes can be legally avoided, reduced, and deferred by using the various exemptions in the tax code, thereby giving you money to use to accumulate wealth.

One other suggestion about taxes. The IRS generally has three years after the filing of a return or two years after the taxes are paid, whichever is later, to call for an audit. If there was an understatement of income of at least 25%, the IRS has six years to start an audit. If you filed a fraudulent return or failed to file, there is no time limit. So keep tax records for at least six years. The general recommendation is to keep your tax returns for 7 years.

In the mid-1930s, Judge Learned Hand wrote a maxim in a famous Appeals Court decision. He wrote, "Anyone may so arrange his affairs that his taxes shall be as low as possible. He is not bound to choose that pattern that best pays the Treasury. Everyone does it, rich and poor alike, and all do right; for nobody owes any public duty to pay more than the law demands."

Even the IRS lives by that practice. In 1992, Congress passed an energy policy law that contained an obscure provision requiring workers who receive free or subsidized parking from their employers to pay income tax on any value above $155 a month. The purpose of the provision was to raise a small amount of revenue while conserving energy and reducing pollution by discouraging commuters from driving to work. Eventually, the IRS in Washington realized that this law applied to them. Panic ensued. The law would cost top IRS executives more than $800 apiece in new taxes each year. After months of fretting, the agency found a way to sidestep the tax. They decided that parking spaces would no longer be reserved in their names. Under the new procedure, the IRS officials will continue to be guaranteed free parking in one of the 79 spaces in the small garage under the IRS headquarters, but they may not be able to park in the same spot every day.

What's good for the goose is good for the gander!

MY ACTION PLAN: CHOOSING A TAX STRATEGY

To avoid paying more than necessary in taxes, develop a tax strategy that includes the following suggestions.

Step 1: Do not Get a Tax Refund

Do not get a tax refund! Most who do think they are doing well. They are not. Think about it. You give Uncle Sam hundreds, maybe thousands, of dollars for "him" to keep and use for a year or more. That's an interest-free loan! In the meantime, you *lose* purchasing power because of inflation. Thus, you get back *less* than you paid. So, have your paycheck adjusted so that, come next April 15th, you do not owe anything and do not get a refund. If you invest the extra money you will have every month from not overpaying, you can make money on interest instead of giving Uncle Sam a tax-free loan.

Step 2: If Possible, Avoid Taxes

There are not many ways to avoid taxes. Borrowing money from the cash value in an insurance policy is a tax-free maneuver, but it is a long-term strategy.

Frankly, the tax-exempt options work best for people in higher tax brackets. To determine if a tax-exempt investment is better than a taxable investment for you, calculate the after-tax return of the taxable investment and compare it to the tax-exempt investment. This is done by first subtracting your tax bracket from 1 and then multiplying that figure by your taxable income. For example, suppose you are in a 36% tax bracket and must choose between a taxable investment yielding 9% and a tax-exempt investment yielding 6%. Subtract .36 from one (1-.36=.64) and then multiply the result (.64) times the taxable yield (9% x .64=5.76%). The 5.76% is what you would get on a 9% investment after you paid taxes. So if you can get 5.76% or higher on a tax-exempt investment, do it. The chart below shows the after-tax returns for a 9% and a 10% investment in each of the several tax brackets (keep in mind that tax brackets change).

Tax bracket	**15%**	**28%**	**31%**	**36%**	**39.60%**
9% after taxes	7.65%	6.48%	6.21%	5.76%	5.44%
10% after taxes	8.50%	7.20%	6.90%	6.40%	6.04%

As you can see, a tax-exempt investment is more likely to outperform a taxable investment for people in the higher tax brackets. The risk should be considered. The tax-exempt investment may have a lower risk, making the slightly lower return more desirable to some investors.

Step 3: Take All Possible Deductions

If you haven't done so already and you want a tax deduction, purchase a home. For the average American, the biggest tax deduction is the interest paid on a home mortgage. For other deductions, study Schedule A carefully, including the IRS booklet that explains them. Even if you have a full-time job, consider starting a business. Schedule C lists all the business expenses that can be deducted from business income.

Step 4: Take Advantage of Tax Deferral

Money in some insurance policies, annuities, and retirement plans grows tax-deferred. This is a long-term strategy, but it does work and should be used.

For example, here is an illustration of two accounts: one is tax-deferred and the other is not. Both accounts assume a 12% return. The taxable account assumes a 28% tax bracket. (This is a hypothetical investment and does not represent any particular investment.)

Years of Growth	Taxed at 28%	Tax deferred
5	12,911	14,230
10	22,565	28,603
15	34,150	50,409
20	51,682	88,838
25	78,215	156,563
30	118,369	275,917
35	179,138	486,261
40	271,105	856,958
43	347,622	1,203,964

The facts speak for themselves.

Chapter 8

THE FAST LANE

To accelerate wealth, you need to invest. In one of His parables, Jesus used investing as an illustration. He told of a wealthy man who said to one of his servants, "You ought to have deposited my money with the bankers, and at my coming, I would have received back my own with interest" (Matthew 25:27). Jesus was saying He wanted as much return as possible on His investment. In financial terms today, that means not just putting money in the bank; it means investing! In terms of the road analogy, this could be called getting into the fast lane because with proper investments, your money grows faster.

The word "invest" means "to commit money to gain profit." The idea behind "saving" is to set aside money for future use. When you save money, you want it to be safe and quickly available for use. That's called liquidity. The concept behind investments is profit. When you invest money, you want it to grow. When you are saving, where you put the money is simple:

somewhere safe, such as a government-insured bank account or a money market account. When you invest, you put your money somewhere to grow, but there is no guarantee; there is a risk. So there are questions you should ask before you invest. What are those questions?

Why Invest?

To Make Money The first and foremost answer is: in the future, you will need more money than you would have if you had saved it in a low-yielding, safe account. That means you must invest and reinvest what you make on the investment. Making money is *the purpose* of investments. Granted, investments may not be as safe as a bank savings account. A ship is safe in port, but ships are not made to sit in a port.

To Protect Against Inflation Supply and demand cause prices to increase or decrease. The rate of inflation varies from year to year, but it is always rising. According to the Department of Labor, the *average* yearly inflation rate from 1976 to 1995 was above 5%. In other words, what $1000 would buy in 1976 costs $2756 in 1995. For example, a first-class postage stamp in 1976 cost ten cents. In 1995, that same stamp cost 32 cents. Prices will increase. Below is a chart showing the effects of inflation on $1,000 at various average annual rates from 10 to 40 years.

Effects of inflation on $1,000

Years	4%	5%	6%
10	$1,480	$1,629	$1,791
20	$2,191	$2,653	$3,207
30	$3,243	$4,322	$5,743
40	$4,801	$7,040	$10,286

The point is that money in a savings account earning 2% or less does not protect against inflation. Money in an insured account avoids the risk of loss, but at such low interest rates, it does not sidestep the risk of inflation. To beat inflation over time, you *must* invest in something that will yield a better return than a savings account.

To Avoid Taxes If you can invest in something that is tax-deferred, your money will grow faster for the simple reason that you will not only have the money you did not pay in taxes, but you will also be able to earn interest on that money.

Thus, the ABC's of investment purposes are **a**voiding taxes, **b**eating inflation, and **c**ontrolling risk while making money. These apply to every investor. The general objectives for investments are to avoid taxes as much as legally possible and to beat inflation as much as possible while at the same time making as much money as your risk tolerance level will allow you. In short, minimize risk; maximize return.

What are the Possible Investments?

The number of possible investments is large. A book titled *The New York Times Complete Guide to Personal Investing* provides a brief overview of a wide range of possibilities. Each investment covers only 4 or 5 pages, yet there are more than 600 pages in the book! And it does not list all the possibilities! All the possibilities, or even a few, in any detail, cannot be discussed here, but at least an introduction to the basics is given.

When you have money that you want to use to earn more money, there are only two basic things you can do with it. You can lend it and earn interest, or buy something hoping it will increase in value so you can sell it at a profit. Assuming, then, that you want to make money with your money, you can put it in a bank account, in real estate, in an insurance product, in tangible assets, or in securities.

Bank Accounts There are different types of bank accounts. Putting your money in a savings account at your local bank is simple and convenient. Your money is also liquid, meaning you can get cash easily and quickly, and it's guaranteed. In 1933, Congress established the Federal Deposit Insurance Corporation to insure bank deposits. At a FDIC-insured bank, deposits are insured up to a limit. Ask your bank what the current limit is. Deposits in a savings account earn interest. The downside is that the returns on a savings account are so low that they generally do not keep up with inflation. This, however, is a good place to start saving.

A Certificate of Deposit (CD) is a glorified savings account. The depositor puts a specific amount of money in a CD at a stated rate of interest for a specified period. Maturities range from a month to five years or longer. CDs are safe. At a FDIC-insured bank, deposits are insured to a limit. CDs pay a higher interest rate than a savings account, but the returns are so low that they generally do not keep up with inflation. (They're called "Certificates of Depreciation.") Furthermore, the money is tied up for the length of time specified in the contract, there are penalties for premature withdrawals, and the interest earned is subject to federal, state, and possibly local taxes.

Real Estate After putting money in a bank account, we usually invest in a house we call home. This is an excellent idea because over your lifetime, the property will probably appreciate (though it might not), meaning you may make money on a necessary living expense. Moreover, you save on taxes. Interest paid on a home mortgage is deductible. Homeownership is not the only type of real estate investment. Two other possibilities (and there are others) are rental property and vacant land. As with all investments, there are risks. The hassle of the castle is paint and plumbing. With rental property, it is tenants and toilets. With vacant land, you have to pay taxes, an expense, while there may be no income.

Insurance As we have seen, it is possible to put money in a permanent type of life insurance policy. The advantages are that the money grows tax-deferred and, in some policies, the cash value can be borrowed at an interest-free loan.

Insurance companies also offer annuities. The dictionary definition of an annuity is "periodic payments of money." In a sense, an annuity is the opposite of an insurance policy. Life insurance is a contract with an insurance company whereby you pay premiums and, upon your death, a death benefit is paid. A cash estate is created. An annuity is the opposite; it is a contract with an insurance company whereby you make a lump-sum payment (or a series of periodic payments to build up a cash estate), and the insurance company makes periodic payments to you.

The money in an annuity grows tax-deferred. If money is withdrawn within a set number of years, usually the first seven, the insurance company applies a graded surrender charge. Withdrawals before age 59½ are subject to a 10% penalty tax by the government. Furthermore, withdrawals are taxed as ordinary income to the extent that they exceed the investment.

Tangible Assets There are several types of tangible assets. The precious metals are, of course, primarily gold and silver. Gold is an internationally accepted standard of wealth. It does not respond to supply-and-demand factors in the same way as other commodities do. Psychological, political, and economic factors tend to influence the price of gold. Gold prices tend to rise when fear is a major factor, when political tensions flare, when inflation heats up, and when the dollar declines. Gold glitters brightest when the economic outlook is darkest, that is, when traditional investments like stocks and bonds are threatened. Silver, as an investment, has long stood in gold's shadow, but, unlike gold, it is primarily an industrial metal with many more commercial applications. For example, it is used in making mirrors.

The category of tangible assets called collectibles is endless. The focus of serious investors in collectibles is antiques, art, oriental rugs, or rare coins, but the category includes stamps, rare books, comic books, baseball cards, and even vintage wines.

Securities: Then, there are securities, the types of investments most people think of when they hear the word investment. This area is vast. You need to understand at least some of the basic types of financial investments called "securities."

1. Money Market. A Money Market Fund is a loan that matures in one year or less. Because of its short maturity, this kind of investment turns into "money" very rapidly, hence the name. (Longer-term obligations, that is, long-term bonds, are called "capital markets.") Money market obligations are usually traded between institutions in large amounts, such as minimums of one million or five million dollars. Money market instruments are securities such as T-bills, commercial paper, and "jumbo CDs" (minimum $100,000). A money market *fund* allows small investors to earn market rates of interest while depositing or withdrawing money at will. Many funds will even allow limited check-writing privileges. A money market fund is a good place for your reserve account and for temporarily parking money.

2. Bond. A bond is a loan agreement (an IOU!). It is a loan to a government unit (the federal, state, or local government), a government agency, or a corporation, with the loan to be repaid

on a fixed schedule of one or more future payments at a fixed rate of interest. Bonds are usually issued for $1,000 at a specific interest rate until a certain date. Bondholders make money on interest, that is, the payment of money for the use of money. All bonds pay a fixed rate of return. Hence, they are often referred to as fixed-income investments.

3. Stock. A stock is a share in a company. When people buy stocks, they literally buy a part of a company. A stockholder is a shareholder, or part-owner, of a company. A stockholder can make money in two ways: 1) periodically, the board of directors may declare a dividend, and 2) the stock may appreciate in value, and when you sell at the higher price, you could make a profit called capital gains. Of course, the board may not declare a dividend, and the stock's value may decline.

4. Mutual fund. A mutual fund is a pool of money professionally managed to achieve a stated objective. In other words, many people put their money into a fund or pool, and a professional manager (for a small percentage of the assets) invests it in accordance with the fund's predetermined objective. The objective may be growth, income, or both. A fund can be diversified across different industries, companies, or securities (e.g., stocks, bonds). Mutual funds are one of the most common ways to get into the stock market, but no mutual fund is guaranteed, not even one offered at a bank.

5. Limited partnership. A business entity can be a sole proprietorship, a partnership, a general partnership, a limited partnership, or a corporation. Each of these has different

characteristics, applications, tax advantages, and disadvantages. In a limited partnership, a general partner manages the venture and has unlimited liability, while limited partners are passive investors (they don't manage, and their liability is limited to their investment). Once a year, the limited partners receive a pro rata share of the partnership's income and losses. The losses may be tax-deductible. Hence, a limited partnership may be considered a tax shelter. This type of investment is long-term and not liquid.

There are numerous ways money grows, including profit, appreciation, interest dividends, and capital gains. In business, money grows through profits, buying low and selling high. Real estate may appreciate over time. Bonds usually pay interest semi-annually. Stocks generally pay quarterly dividends, and if they increase in value, they can also provide capital gain.

What Investment Guidelines Should I Follow?

What follows is an introduction to investment planning. The one area that could and, for the serious investor, should be expanded is the discussion concerning asset allocation.

The Investment Purpose Should Be Settled As we have seen, everyone should consider investing to avoid taxes, to beat inflation, and to make money. Beyond those general purposes, there are personal purposes for investing. Is your personal purpose a reserved account, a down payment on a house, an education fund, retirement, etc.?

Your financial stage of life will probably determine your personal investment purpose(s). Not everyone fits into one of these broad categories, but chances are one will fit your situation. The four financial stages are: 1) Getting started. At this stage, a person needs to cover current expenses, contribute to a reserved account, save for the down payment on a house, begin an education fund, and set up a retirement program. 2) Mid-course. At this stage, individuals must maintain their standard of living, cover college costs, and continue to invest for retirement. 3) Approaching retirement. At this stage, the focus is on minimizing taxes and increasing retirement funding. 4) Retirement. Now, people need to maximize their investment income to keep pace with inflation and protect their estates for their heirs.

The Investment Objective Should Be Set What is the time horizon for your investment program, short-term or long-term? The short term is five years or less. Short-term objectives include establishing a reserved account, saving for a car down payment, and saving for a house down payment. These funds should be in a liquid account. Long term is five years or more. Long-term objectives include saving for college and retirement. These funds could be growth-oriented. In short, is the goal liquidity, short-term accumulation, long-term growth, income, or secure income?

Investment Goals Should Be Stated. Is the goal safety, growth, tax savings, or income? If you are concerned about losing some of the money you invest, safety is your goal. If you are in a high tax bracket, tax savings may be your goal. If you are investing for your children's education, reasonable growth is the goal. If you are investing for retirement, you need long-term gains and, preferably, tax deferment. At retirement, the goal becomes income, not growth.

Obviously, there is some overlap between purpose, objective, and goal. All three are used to help you thoroughly think through your investment approach.

An Investment Plan Should Be Developed Next, you need a plan to meet your goals and objectives that will accomplish your purpose. Your plan should be based on solid financial principles and designed according to a sound financial strategy. The most fundamental financial principles are as follows.

1. The power of compounding. Continuously reinvesting the interest and dividends over a long period of time multiplies money.

2. Tax deferral. Deferring taxes enhances investment returns by making more money available to earn. It assumes that when you retire, you will be in a lower tax bracket.

3. The risk/return trade-off. Investments have different levels of risk. Low-risk investments include FDIC-insured bank accounts, bonds, especially government bonds, the cash value in a whole life or universal life policy that is guaranteed to earn a preset minimum rate, and money markets. Risk increases from there. Moderate risk investments include real estate, some mutual funds, corporate bonds, and blue-chip stocks. High-risk investments include tangible assets, limited partnerships, futures, and options. The following investment pyramid illustrates the concept.

The highest risk, the highest return

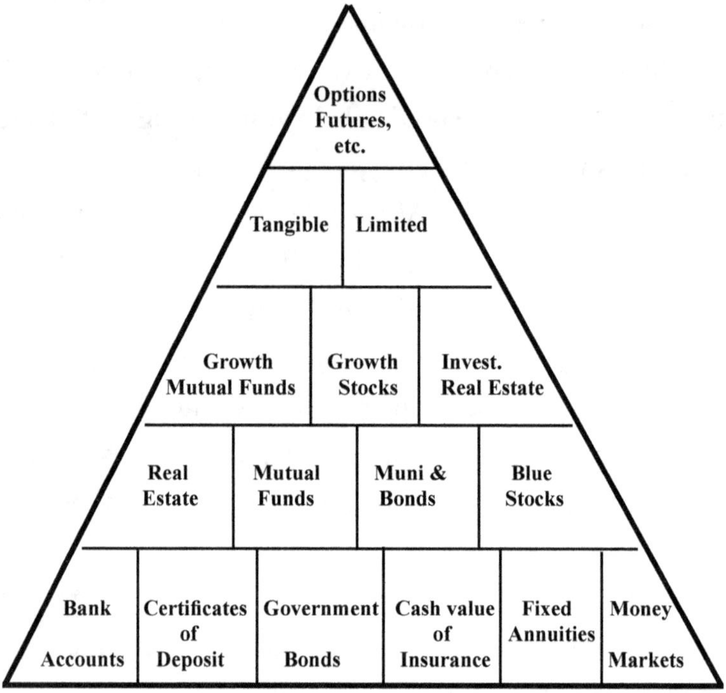

The lowest risk, the lowest return

The pyramid is not exhaustive. Furthermore, some investments could be listed in multiple categories. For example, a particular stock, mutual fund, etc. could be classified as low, medium, or high risk. Investors may differ on where to place an investment on the chart.

Investments have different rates of return. Stocks usually have greater returns than bonds. The risk/return tradeoff is: *the higher the risk, the greater the possible return (or loss).* The investor is paid a higher return for taking the higher risk. The investment pyramid illustrates this.

4. Risk tolerance. Investors have different levels of risk tolerance. Based on their risk tolerance, there are three major investor types.

Conservative investors have a low tolerance for risk. They want to see investments increase steadily in value and do not want to risk losing money in the process. They take lower returns to avoid losses. The most conservative investors desire a *guarantee* that the principal will not be lost. The only guaranteed investment is an insured bank account. The downside is a low return, so low that at times the return does not keep up with inflation.

Moderate investors are willing to accept some risk and a periodic decline in investment value if it may lead to a higher return. In other words, moderate investors are willing to take some risks to achieve desired investment objectives while at the same time seeking an element of security.

Aggressive investors are comfortable with a higher degree of risk. They seek maximum long-term gains with little concern about short-term losses in value. (It is not an actual loss until the investment is sold.) They are willing to take chances to meet investment objectives.

5. Diversification. Diversification reduces risk. This is a cardinal concept. The Greeks never sent all their grain on a single ship. They divided the cargo among several ships and even sent them by different trade routes. If one ship was lost at

sea, the others had a chance of arrival. The ancients knew that diversification lowers the risk of loss.

6. Long-term investing. Time can also reduce risk in some investments.

7. Cost. Investments have different costs. When a person purchases a house, a fee is paid to the realtor. Likewise, there are fees connected to any other investment.

8. Dollar-cost averaging. This is done by investing the same amount at regular intervals regardless of the current price or the market conditions. Dollar-cost averaging is designed to reduce *costs*. The theory is that over time, as prices go up and down, the average cost of all the shares purchased will be lower, because the average cost would not be as high as it would be if all the shares were purchased at the highest price. (On the other hand, the *average* cost will not be as low as it would be if all the shares were purchased at the lowest price, but as the price goes up and down, dollar-cost averaging will reduce the cost because the cost will not be as great as it would be if all the shares were purchased at the highest price.)

The question becomes: with your personal purpose(s), objectives, and goals, as well as these *principles* in mind, what *strategy* should you employ? That is the subject of debate. There are two basic strategies: active (buy low, sell high) and passive (buy and hold). The most well-known active strategy is market timing. The well-known passive strategy is asset allocation.

9. Market timing. One approach to an active strategy is market timing, *constantly* buying and selling. Unless you are

knowledgeable, do not be a *trader* investing only for the short term; be an investor investing long term.

10. Asset allocation. Asset allocation (asset class mix), a theory of a buy-and-hold strategy, insists that investments not only be diversified but also diversified across asset categories or classes. A widely quoted study by Brinson, Hood, and Beebower indicates that, for long-range performance, over 90% of a portfolio's returns are determined by the choice of asset classes and asset allocation rather than by the selection of individual stocks and/or market timing. (See "Determinants of Portfolio Performance," by Gary P. Brinson, L. Randolph Hood, and Gilbert L. Beebower in *Financial Analysts Journal,* July-August, 1986. An update in the May-June 1991 issue overwhelmingly confirmed the conclusion of the earlier study.) The basic asset classes are 1) cash equivalents such as interest-bearing accounts, money market accounts, and treasury bills, 2) bonds, that is, treasury bonds, municipal bonds, and corporate bonds, and 3) stocks.

Asset allocation asks two questions: which assets to include and what percentage of the portfolio to allocate to each class? As you can imagine, there are numerous theories as to how to answer these two questions. The *classic* answer is that a balanced portfolio is 40% bonds and 60% stocks. While virtually all approaches go beyond that simple allocation, most maintain some kind of a split between bonds (and maybe money markets) and stocks.

Two popular approaches determine asset allocation based on

age and risk. An old adage suggests that a person's *age* should match the percentage of the portfolio invested in safe, stable holdings such as money markets, bonds, and fixed-rate annuities, while the remainder is in stocks, etc. For example, according to this idea, people in their 20s would allocate 20% of their portfolio to money markets, bonds, etc., and 80% to stocks. In comparison, people in their 30s would increase the money market and bond allocation to 30%, etc. Professionals usually do not follow such a simplistic approach. The *risk* approach suggests an asset mix based on the level of risk. Conservative investors might allocate 70% to 80% to bonds, 10% to a money market, and 10% to stocks. (That is super conservative!) Moderate investors may allocate 40% to 60% to bonds and money market accounts, and the remainder to equities. Aggressive risk-takers would allocate only 10% to 20% to bonds and the rest to stocks, especially to growth or aggressive-growth funds.

These two approaches to asset allocation are not mutually exclusive; they blend together nicely. Older investors should be more conservative than younger investors. Younger investors can afford the risk of an aggressive approach.

The following examples of "basic asset allocation" demonstrate how asset allocation changes at various financial stages of life or for different investors. None of these examples should be taken as investment advice because every situation is different. *An actual asset allocation should be more detailed.* It would further allocate the bond and stock assets.

Basis Asset Allocation

Conservative (design for income)
80% in bonds and money markets
20% in stocks
Moderate (design for moderate growth)
40% in bonds and money markets
60% in stocks
Aggressive (design for growth)
20% bonds
80% stocks

That is the *classic* approach to asset allocation. Because bonds have yielded such low returns lately, a more *current* approach to asset allocation, especially for a beginner, would be to start with a conservative stock mutual fund. Mutual funds provide diversification, and different classes offer varying levels of risk.

Equity income funds are conservative because they invest in companies that pay dividends. Beyond that are **growth and income** funds, **growth funds**, and **aggressive growth funds**. If you start with a small amount of money or a small monthly investment, begin with an equity income fund. If a larger amount of money is available, put some of it in an equity income fund, some in a growth and income fund, and, depending on your risk tolerance level, some in a growth fund and, perhaps, in an aggressive growth fund.

With the general purpose of investing, your personal purpose, objectives, and risk tolerance in mind, choose an investment strategy. As you can see, this can be a complex process. Candidly, unless you understand asset allocation, you should consult a professional who does.

An Investment Portfolio Should Be Monitored After the plan is in place, the various investments should be monitored. Things change. As you move through the financial stages of life, your purposes, objectives, and goals change. Financial markets change. Tax laws change. A good investment this year may be a miserable investment next year. That does not mean, however, that you should get out of the stock market just because there is a downturn, especially if your investment objective is long-term growth.

Summary: To avoid taxes, beat inflation, and have your money grow so you can accumulate wealth to accomplish your purpose(s), objectives, and goals, you should invest your money based on solid financial principles and designed according to a sound financial strategy.

One word of caution: as you can see, investing can be complicated and tricky. Remember, a little knowledge can be dangerous. I recommend that you commit the time and effort it takes to learn and keep up with investments, or do yourself a favor and find a competent professional.

Whatever you do, invest. Money is green; it grows! You grow a plant by planting a seed, fertilizing and watering it, and letting nature take its course. Similarly, money grows by taking a small amount, planting it in the soil of investment, and letting nature take its course.

At the end of the chapter on banking, the story of the book *The Richest Man in Babylon* was begun. The rest of the story is that the wealthy man told Arkad that having one year's earnings wasn't the whole truth. In his words, "If you become wealthy, then what you save must earn, and its children must earn." So, he concluded that a person should save at least 10% (he added, "Pay yourself first."), live on 90% (i.e., pay cash) and invest what you save. "Wealth," he said, "like a tree, grows from a tiny seed." Your savings are the seed.

Arkad practiced these principles for a year and then discovered there was more to learn. He invested his savings with a brickmaker who had a scheme concerning jewels. He learned the hard way that "He who takes advice about his savings from one who is inexperienced in such matters shall pay with his savings for proving the falsity of their opinions." In other words, "Why trust the knowledge of a brickmaker about jewels?" The jewels turned out to be glass. Arkad had jerked up his wealth tree by the roots. He had to start again. At least he had formed the habit of saving 10%.

There was still more to learn about how money works. The next time he invested wisely and spent the money he had earned from the investment. He was told, "You do eat the children of your savings." His children needed to have children who worked for him. In short, invest the money earned from investments.

From this wealthy man, Arkad mastered the three laws of managing wealth successfully. He was told, "You first learned to live upon less than you could earn. Next, you learned to seek advice from those who were competent through their own experience to give it, and, lastly, you have learned to make gold work for you." He had learned how to earn money, keep it, and use it.

MY ACTION PLAN: FOLLOWING AN INVESTMENT PLAN

If you are to accumulate wealth of any size, you must, at some point, invest money to make money. Let's assume that at the moment, you are not investing at all or, worse yet, you are in debt. Let's start from the very beginning and build an investment plan.

Step 1: Establish a Reserved Account

You need to establish a reserved account. Most financial planners would probably say you need six months of living expenses in an emergency account. I have heard professionals suggest from three months for some to one year for self-employed people. If you do not have such an account, you should *open one immediately, even if you can only put a small amount* in it. Open a savings account (or use an existing one) and start putting money in it that you will only use in an emergency.

Having a reserved account is *part* of an investment plan. If you have all your extra money tied up in investments and an emergency arises, you might be caught in a situation where you have to sell at a loss. So you need a reserved account *before* you have an investment fund. The point is that investments need time to grow. You should invest only money you will not need for some time. So, before you invest, build an emergency fund. After you reach the six-month amount (or whatever figure you decide), the money you are putting into the reserved account can be directed to your investment portfolio.

Step 2: Obtain Life Insurance

You should also have life insurance before you invest. Life insurance on the breadwinner(s) is family income protection. If you put $100 per month into an investment and die one year later, your family will have $1200 plus whatever the investment has earned. On the other hand, if you put $100 per month into an insurance policy and one year later you die, your family would have many times what an investment for that amount you have yielded. The difference between the two might be as much as $100,000!

For anyone with responsibilities, like a spouse or children, life insurance is *part* of a sound financial plan. In fact, if you have responsibilities, you need insurance even before getting out of debt. If you wait until you get out of debt before you get insurance, you may die first!

Step 3: Get out of Debt

Okay, now, if you are in debt, do everything you can to get totally out of debt. See the chapter on credit, especially the action plan at the end, for specific suggestions. If you are deep in debt, you are paying hundreds and, perhaps, thousands of dollars in interest, not to mention the payments themselves, that you could be saving and investing. This does not mean you have to be totally out of debt before you begin an investment plan, but obviously, the more debt-free you are, the more you can invest.

Although, as a general rule, these first three steps are in the right order, admittedly, they are not necessarily the right order for everyone. For example, depending on your individual situation, you may deem it prudent to get life insurance first.

Step 4: Implement an Investment Plan

The following questions should be thought through and answered *on paper*.

1. What is your personal purpose(s) for investing?
   - Is the purpose a reserved account?
   - Is it a down payment on a house?
   - Is it an education fund?
   - Is it money for retirement?
2. What is the financial objective (time frame) for your investment program?
   - Is the objective liquidity?
   - Is the objective short-term accumulation?
   - Is the objective long-term growth?
3. What is the financial goal?
   - Is the goal safety?
   - Is the goal tax saving?
   - Is the goal income?
   - Is the goal growth?

4. What is your financial plan?
    What is your risk tolerance?
    Are you a conservative investor?
    Are you a moderate investor?
    Are you an aggressive investor?
    What is your investment strategy?
    What is your asset allocation?
    What percentage of the portfolio is to be in each asset?

If you do not have much money to invest or only have a small sum you could invest each month, then, depending on your risk tolerance, begin with a mutual fund, such as an equity fund or a growth and income fund. You can open a mutual fund account for as little as a $100 lump sum or $25 per month. Actually, you can open some mutual funds for nothing.

On the other hand, if you have a large sum, you either need to invest a great deal of time in studying before you invest your money, or you need to seek the services of a professional stockbroker or a financial advisor who practices asset allocation.

Chapter 9

LOOKING DOWN THE ROAD

On the road to accelerating wealth, there comes the time to slow down and enjoy what you have accomplished. If investment is the fast lane, perhaps retirement is the slow lane. For those not yet there, it is looking down the road.

People dream about retirement. They imagine how wonderful it would be not to have to go to work next week, next month, next year—never again. If you ask people of all ages what they want to do when they retire, the vast majority will say “travel.”

Unfortunately, most dream; few do serious retirement planning. You should dream, but don’t live in a dream world. If all you do is dream about retirement now, those years could easily be a nightmare.

If your dreams are to come true, you must be wide awake. That’s true about any future dream you might have, but it is especially true concerning retirement. One of the main motives for managing your money now and accumulating wealth is retirement. There are realities about retirement that you must face now if you are to enjoy retirement later. What are these retirement realities?

Your Retirement Length Will Be Longer Than You Think

The first retirement reality concerns how long you will live. More than likely, this is a subject you have not given much thought to.

What We Think How long do you think you will live? Many have been conditioned to think that their retirement years will be relatively short. They hear that we have three score years and ten and assume they will live to be about 70, which is only five years after 65, the traditional retirement age. They hear that our genes determine the length of our lives. Most have parents who didn't live past 75 or so, and therefore assume they will only live about that long.

The Reality The reality is that three score and ten years is no longer true today, and while there is some truth to the idea that our genes determine the length of life, many live longer than their parents. There are a number of reasons people live longer today, including better diets, more exercise, and advanced medical technology, such as organ transplants. Studies indicate that people are living 26% longer than 20 years ago. The average woman today lives to 81.4 years, and the average man lives to 76.5 years. The chances are very good you could live to be 85 and, if our knowledge continues to increase, you could live to be 90 or 95.

Your Retirement Cost Will Be More Than You Imagine

The second retirement reality concerns how much it takes to live when you retire. If we have not thought seriously about how long we will live, we have probably given even less thought to how much it will cost to live that long.

What We Think How much do you think it will cost per year for you to live when you retire? We typically either don't think about it at all or we think only in vague terms. We assume our house will be paid for and conclude that it will not cost us nearly as much to live there as it does now. People in Southern California think they can radically cut their living expenses by moving to a rural area or out of state. When they see a retired couple doing something like that today, it confirms their assumptions.

The Reality The reality is that while it may be true that your house is paid for, the cost per year for you to live during retirement will be greater than most imagine, no matter where you live. The reason is inflation! Inflation drives the cost of living to unbelievable heights.

In 1970, a financial advisor told me that the average income in 1939 was $1,500 a year. (I remember that because that's the year I was born.) Then he said that, because of inflation, maintaining that same standard of living in 1970 would cost $10,000. (I remember that because that's what I was making that year!) He went on to tell me that if inflation continued at expected rates, it would take $90,000 a year to maintain the same lifestyle in retirement. I am amazed at how close he was.

If you are as old as I am, it is not hard to conceive. I paid $15,000 for my first house. (I actually bought two houses for that price. There were two houses on one lot.) My mortgage payment was $100 per month, and the interest rate was 6% fixed. Seven years later, I paid $34,500 for a house with a $325 monthly payment. Five years after that, I paid $159,000 for a comparable house in another part of the country, and my payments jumped to $ 1,226.06 per month at 10% interest, which was a very good deal at the time. I remember when gas was 23.9 cents a gallon and when I could buy a hamburger and a Coke for 30 cents. Inflation is the reason your retirement is going to cost more than you think.

A modern Rip Van Winkle slept for 20 years. When he woke up, he called his broker immediately. “What’s the stock market done in the last 20 years?” he inquired. With the aid of a computer, his broker soon reported that his 100 shares of A.T.&T. were now worth $9.5 million, his 100 shares of General Motors were worth $7.9 million, and his oil holdings had increased to $19 million. “Great!” Rip exclaimed, “I’m rich!” At which point the telephone operator interrupted and said, “Your three minutes are up, sir. Please deposit one million dollars.”

Your Retirement Resources Will Be Less Than You Assume

The third retirement reality concerns any financial plans you have for retirement.

What We Think When asked about their specific retirement plan, people say things like "I've not given it much thought," "I have Social Security," "I have a plan at work." They seem to think that a combination of social security and their plan at work will be sufficient.

The Reality The reality is that, more than likely, your retirement resources will be less than you assume. When people who have a plan are asked, "What exactly will you receive?" they usually don't know. They assume that because they have a plan, it will work out somehow.

Will Social Security be sufficient for you? In the first place, Social Security was never meant to be the complete source of income for anyone's retirement. Furthermore, many are questioning what the future of Social Security will be like. Some even suggest that the system will be bankrupt. That may be extreme. If the system survives, will it be enough for you? Would you like to be living solely on Social Security now?

What about your plan at work? If you have one and you get it, it will certainly help. There are, however, two major problems with relying on the employer-sponsored retirement plan.

First, will you actually get it? Several things could prevent that like 1) not being vested (that is, you have to be employed X number of years to qualify or fully qualify to receive retirement payments, 2) changing jobs and, therefore, not having the plan that you thought you would and, 3) the company not existing for one reason or another, including going out of business, being taken over, or you being laid off because your position is no longer needed.

Second, you may keep your job at your company and actually receive retirement checks, only to discover they are less than you need to enjoy retirement.

If your plan is a combination of Social Security and a plan at work, you will obviously be better off than someone with only Social Security, but are you sure that what you will receive from both sources will be sufficient for you to enjoy your retirement years?

After looking at his projected retirement income, one fellow concluded, "I have enough money to last me the rest of my life—provided I walk across freeways."

You *can* outlive your money!

Summary: The length, cost, and resources of your retirement will not be what you think. The realities of retirement are that you will live longer, it will cost more, and your resources will be less than you have assumed, which means you must accumulate wealth now for retirement later.

MY ACTION PLAN: SELECTING A RETIREMENT PLAN

Calculating what you will need for retirement sounds simple. Just determine how much you will need to live on during retirement and how much you will have to invest now to arrive at that amount later. The problem is that all attempts to arrive at what your actual need will be are based on assumptions such as your personal monthly retirement income need, the inflation rate between now and your retirement, the length of your retirement, the inflation rate during your retirement, your social security payment, your pension payment, your personal savings, etc. The conclusions are only as correct as the assumptions are accurate. The best way to determine what you need to invest now for retirement later is to use a computer program that will start with your need for retirement in today's dollars and, based on all the above-mentioned assumptions, calculate what that amount will be at your retirement. You really should talk to a professional financial advisor who specializes in retirement planning.

Now, having said that, there are things you can and should do. This exercise is designed only to give you a very rough estimate of your future retirement needs.

Step 1: Calculate the Retirement Income Desired

As a general rule, experts say you will need 80% of your current income or 70% of your average income in the last five years before retirement to maintain your present standard of living during retirement. That, of course, does not take into account inflation between now and the time you retire.

So, to give you some idea of the need, assume you said that you would need $2500 a month in today's dollars to maintain your current standard of living during retirement. The chart below shows the effects of inflation at various average yearly rates over periods of 10 to 40 years.

Effects of inflation on $2,500

Years	**4%**	**5%**	**6%**
10	$3,701	$4,072	$4,477
20	$5,478	$6,633	$8,018
30	$8,108	$10,805	$14,359
40	$12,003	$17,600	$25,714

As you can see, inflation greatly increases the amount of money you will need at retirement. That is only the beginning. The amount you came up with for a monthly need *at* retirement does not include how much you will need *for* retirement. To determine that, you need to make some assumptions about how long you will live, what the inflation rate will be during those years, and how much of your money you want left over when you die.

Step 2: Estimate your Retirement Income

You should put together a plan that includes Social Security, any plan you may have at work, plus a personal investment program.

Social Security Social Security alone may not be sufficient, but every little bit helps. First, you should find out what Social Security says you will receive when you retire. To get a free copy of your Personal Earnings and Benefit Estimate Statement, call 1 (800) 772-1213.

By the way, you should periodically check your Social Security statement by comparing it with your W-2s. Mistakes can happen. Furthermore, millions of people use fake Social Security numbers so that someone may be using your number. Mistakes on your record can be costly because your benefits later are determined by what is recorded now. The statute of limitations for an appeal is three years, three months, and three days from the contested year.

A Pension Plan at Work Your plan at work will also help. It is either a defined-benefit plan (a traditional plan) or a defined-contribution plan.

Defined benefits plans provide a "pre-defined" or guaranteed income for life. If you have a traditional pension plan at work, ask the benefits office to give you an estimate of what you will receive at retirement. As a rule, if you work for 20 years, you will get 40% to 50% of your salary for life.

Traditional plans are rapidly being replaced by defined contribution plans, such as 401(k) plans, that often require you to make investment choices. If the plan at work matches your contribution, put in as much as you need to get the maximum match. That's free money. Also, if you have choices, choose diversification and growth. An employer-sponsored retirement plan, such as a 401(k), includes a booklet that explains the plan and its asset allocation. Read it. If you do not understand the material on diversification (asset allocation), read the chapter on investments in this book again, then the booklet from your plan at work again. If you still feel you do not understand, ask a professional to explain them to you until you do. You must understand this concept. It could cost you thousands of dollars if you do not.

Here's the problem. People who do not understand investments in general, or asset allocation in particular, read the booklet from work, see words like "guaranteed," "safe," "low risk," and, feeling they do not want to lose money, put all their money into conservative accounts. That may be appropriate in some cases, but for a younger person, that kind of investment strategy could result in thousands of dollars less at retirement than they would have with proper asset allocation.

Your retirement plan booklet from work should give you examples of conservative, moderate, and growth strategies for investing. (Also, see the material on asset allocation on page 97.) If you are in your 20s, 30s, or 40s, you should choose a growth mix of investments in your retirement plan.

If you have a 401(k), 403(b), etc., at work, ask the benefits office to give you an estimate of what you will receive at retirement. Determining the final figure is difficult because all estimates are based on your contributions that could change and on the assumed rate of return on your investment. Be conservative.

A Personal Plan Beyond Social Security and whatever plan you may have at work, you need a personal plan. The plan you choose depends on your type of employment, any plan you have at work, and the tax consequences. Because of government regulations, this is one of the most complicated areas of financial planning. You should definitely consult a professional.

If you qualify, open an IRA. An IRA is a plan that allows you to put money into a retirement account and deduct that amount from your current taxes. There is a limit to the amount that can be put into such an account. Since the limit changes periodically, check with an account to determine the current limit. The money in the IRA grows tax-deferred. You will pay taxes on the money as it is withdrawn during your retirement years. Because the rules are based on the retirement plan offered at your work and your tax bracket, you need to either know the rules or consult a professional.

Better yet, open a Roth IRA. In a Roth IRA, you have to put in money that you have already paid taxes on, but the investments in a Roth IRA grow tax-deferred, and when you retire, you take it all out tax-free! Like the IRS, there is a limit to the amount that can be put into a Roth IRA, and the limit changes periodically. So check with an account to determine the current limit.

If you have used all the options for qualified retirement plans with tax-deferred growth, such as a 401(k), 403(b), an IRA, etc., consider an annuity.

If you need insurance, seriously consider a life insurance policy that provides for a tax-deferred build-up that can also be withdrawn, under certain conditions, tax-free. For example, universal life and variable universal life provide insurance and tax deferral, which, under some circumstances, also provide tax-free withdrawals.

Step 3: Determine what you need to invest for retirement

As has been explained, because of the many assumptions, determining what you need to invest for retirement is difficult. You should consult a professional with a computer program designed for this task. Studies indicate that people are only saving about one-third of what they should be saving for retirement. Don't delay; start today.

Chapter 10

THE END OF THE ROAD

At the end of the road of the financial journey is death. Common sense reminds us of the bad news. The statistics are in: one out of one dies! That is the bad news. The Scripture recognized that and adds the good news. It says, "It is appointed for men to die once, but after this the judgment, so Christ was offered once to bear the sins of many" (Hebrews 9:27-28). The gospel, a Greek word that means "good news," is that Jesus Christ died for our sins and rose from the dead (1 Corinthians 15:1-5). All who trust Him to get them to heaven are given eternal life in heaven as a gift (John 3:16; Romans 6:23).

If you have mastered money management during your life, you will leave money behind when you die. Planning who gets what is left is called estate planning. To most, the expression "estate planning" sounds like something wealthy people do. Granted, the rich need to do estate planning, but so do the not-so-rich.

When most hear the word "estate," they think of a massive mansion on a large lot with a high wall around it. That may be the popular impression of an estate, but that is not the only meaning of the word. Another meaning of the word "estate" is possessions. One of the dictionary definitions of "estate" is "all of one's possessions, especially those left by a deceased person." If you have possessions, you have an estate! What do you possess? Do you have money in a bank account? Do you own property? Do you have financial assets? If you have any of these, you have an estate.

When you die, everything you have, your estate, will be left here. As the proverb reminds us, "You can't take it with you." If you have minor children, you will leave them in the custody and care of someone else. If you own anything, ownership will be transferred to someone else. The prospect of your death raises the question, "Who gets the wealth you have accumulated over your lifetime?"

That question may not be as simple as it seems. Several things could prevent all of your estate from going to those you wish. If you do not legally choose a guardian for your minor children and you and your spouse (both natural parents) die, the state will choose the guardian of your children! If you do not legally determine who gets your possessions, the state will decide who the new owner of your assets is.

Furthermore, when a person dies, state laws govern the *transfer* of property. In California, state laws say that if you have possessions in your name worth over $208,850, when you die, your estate must go through probate court, a special court that handles the distribution of the property of deceased people. (as of 2026. That figure changes periodically. So check the current amount.) For these purposes, the value of your house is determined by its market value, not by the amount of the equity you have in it, which means that if you own a house worth $500,000 and your equity is only $1, since the market value is over $208,850, your estate must go to probate court.

Then, there are the federal tax laws. When you die, your estate must file a final income tax return. Your estate could have to pay an estate tax! Estate taxes can be very expensive. Moreover, they are due in nine months in cash, which means that your estate might have to sell an asset to pay estate taxes!

You, however, not the government, can control what happens. Probate can be avoided. In some cases, capital gains on a greatly appreciated asset can be entirely eliminated. While if estate taxes are due, they can be reduced. All of this will take some planning.

So, if *you* are to pick the guardian of your minor children, if *you* are to decide who gets what possession or asset, if *your estate* is to avoid probate, or if *your estate* is to pay as little as possible in taxes, *you* have to do some estate planning, which is nothing more than planning for who will get what's left when you die.

There are three ways an estate can be distributed: intestate (not having a will), by a will, and through a trust. Beyond those legal factors, if estate taxes are due, there is a way to provide for them to be paid.

Intestate

If you do not have a will when you die, your estate is distributed "intestate," a word that means "not disposed of by a legal will." If you die intestate, the laws of the state determine how the property is divided.

In California, if you are married when you die and do not have a will, everything goes to your spouse, provided you and your spouse hold your assets as community property. If you do not have a will and you and your mate die at the same time, the probate judge will name a guardian for your minor children, dispose of your property according to the state laws of intestacy, and appoint an administrator who will charge your estate a fee. Either you decide now before you die who will get what, or the probate court will decide for you after you die. Doing nothing is not a plan. The consequences may not be to your liking and could cost your estate thousands of dollars.

Wills

A will is simply a list of instructions that tells the probate judge exactly how you want your estate distributed. Everyone who has specific preferences about how their estate is distributed should have a will.

A will allows *you*, instead of the laws of the state, to determine who gets your possessions. It allows you to name a guardian for your minor children, allocate your property as you wish rather than rely on the provisions of state law, and appoint an executor. Do the children split the estate equally? Is there a particular item or amount of money you want an individual child, relative, friend, charity, or church to have? To ensure that your assets go to those you wish, you need a will.

A will, however, will not solve all the problems. Even if you have a will, your estate still has to go through probate, and that can be time-consuming and expensive.

Probate is the court-administered process by which one's assets are assembled, and one's debts are paid or discharged. Once statutory requirements are satisfied, the estate is distributed to the people entitled to the property. So what's the problem with that?

Delays For one thing, probate means delays. In California, going through probate takes 9 to 18 months. Sometimes assets can be frozen. During the probate process, nothing can be distributed or sold without the court's approval. If your family needs money for living expenses, they will either have to ask the probate court for a living allowance or wait until the probate process is completed, which, as we have seen, takes 9 to 18 months. If the trust is complex or contested probate can take two to three years.

Dollars Another problem with probate is dollars. Probate costs money. If you have a will, you can designate a person or persons to act as "executor." If there is no will, an "administrator" will be appointed by the probate court. (The functions of an executor and an administrator are essentially the same.) The executor (or administrator) and their attorney are entitled to a "statutory commission" for their services. The fee is based on the total gross value of the estate before deducting liabilities. For example, the fees are based on the market value of your house, not the equity you have in it. According to the California Probate Code sections 10800 and 10810, the executor commissions and attorneys' fees are as follows:

4% of the first $100,000
3% of the next $100,000
2% of the next $800,000
1% of the next $9,000,000
½ of 1% of the next $15,000,000
all above $25,000,000"reasonable" amount to bedetermined by the court

Any way you figure it, probate costs money. If you have any size estate at all, meaning if you own a house, it could easily cost thousands.

Disclosure Another problem with probate is disclosure. Probate records are public records available to anyone. The net worth, the debts, and the beneficiaries are all matters of public record. This is not a problem for everyone, but it is for some.

All of these problems and expenses, the delays, dollars, and disclosure of probate, are completely eliminated by having a living trust.

Trusts

A trust is a legal concept. The basic idea is that property is given to a "trustee" who is responsible for administering it for someone else's benefit. A trust can be revocable, meaning it can be changed, or it can be irrevocable, which means it cannot be changed.

A Revocable Living Trust A Revocable Living Trust is a changeable trust administered while you are living and continues according to your wishes, after your death. A trust transfers the property out of your name before you die, but still leaves you in control. Think of a trust as a box in which you place all your possessions. This legal box owns everything in it.

When people first hear this idea, they get nervous. They don't like the thought of losing control of their property. Don't worry. You own and control the box! Living Trusts are normally set up so that the Trustors (the people placing assets in the trust) are the trustees (the people controlling the trust). In a Revocable Living Trust, the assets are still in your name, and since you are normally the only beneficiary of the trust while you are alive, you are also the *beneficiary* owner. Instead of the deed to your house saying John and Jane Doe, it will read something like "John and Jane Doe, Co-trustees of the Doe Revocable Trust." Furthermore, a Living Trust is revocable; you can change it anytime. In other words, practically speaking, nothing happens until you die. A Living Trust enables you to do a number of things.

1. It can give control of your assets to the person of your choice should you become disabled or incompetent.

2. It allows you to avoid probate. When you die, there is nothing to probate (unless you didn't put it in the trust) because

you didn't *personally* hold legal title to anything in the trust. (You held beneficiary title.)

3. It can facilitate the reduction of capital gains tax by holding your assets as community property. A Living Trust may eliminate capital gains on your house (or any other appreciated asset).

In a Living Trust, property can be held as community property instead of joint tenancy with the right of survivorship. This is an important feature for tax purposes. For tax purposes, property has a "basis," which is the original cost. (Actually, the basis is the original cost, less any depreciation that has been taken against the asset since its purchase, plus any capital improvements that have been added to the asset since its purchase.) When the property is sold, everything above the cost basis is taxed as capital gains.

For example, suppose a couple bought a house for $100,000 and over the years it appreciated to the value of $300,000. If they divorced and each sold his or her half, the IRS would say that the cost basis is $100,000 and $200,000 is subject to capital gains. In this case, each would pay capital gains on $100,000, but what would happen if one spouse died? It would depend on how the title of the house was held. If they held the house as joint tenants with the right of survivorship (in which case, for tax purposes, the IRS deems that each spouse *separately* holds a half-interest in the house), the surviving spouse would receive a one-half step up in basis. (This is because, for tax purposes, the deceased spouses' half interest in the property is included in his or her estate *at its fair market value on the date* of his or her death. Thus, the decedent's half interest in the property is *increased* to its fair market value for purposes of adjusting the basis of the property. The survivor's half interest in the property for basis purposes, however, is not affected.) In this scenario, the cost basis is $200,000 and the surviving spouse would have to pay capital gains on $100,000 when the property is sold.

On the other hand, if the same couple held their house as community property and one of them died, the surviving spouse would receive a full step-up in basis, meaning that as far as the IRS is concerned, the cost basis is now $300,000 and there would be no capital gains tax due if the property is sold at the same value it had when the first spouse died.

Therefore, to take advantage of the full step-up in basis, a couple should hold their property as "community property." A Living Trust can accomplish this by changing the title of the property to community property prior to its transfer into the living trust. (Property can be held as community property without being in a Living Trust, but holding property as community property outside a Living Trust does not avoid probate.)

4. It simplifies taking advantage of the unified tax credit. The federal tax code contains an estate tax. When you die and leave your property to someone else, that individual does not have to pay income taxes on what is received, but the estate has to pay estate taxes. A certain amount is exempt, but after that exemption threshold, the estate tax applies. It must be paid in nine months in cash. A Living Trust does not eliminate the

estate tax, but it can reduce this tax. For the current information concerning whether or not your estate will be subject to estate tax and, if so, how a Living Trust can help reduce that tax, consult a lawyer, preferably one who specializes in Living Trusts.

5. It can enable you to control your assets long after you die. You can accomplish this with a will, but the will would have to go through probate before a trust could be established. With a Living Trust, assets can be distributed years later without going through probate.

An Irrevocable Charitable Remainder Trust The second kind of trust in estate planning is an Irrevocable Charitable Remainder Trust. As the title suggests, it is irrevocable, meaning that once it is established, it cannot be changed. As the title also suggests, after all is said and done, a "charity remains," meaning a charity gets what's left.

Here's how it works. You set up an Irrevocable Remainder Trust and transfer an appreciated asset into it. You name yourself as the income beneficiary and one or more qualified charities as "remainderman." The trustee sells the asset, paying no capital gains and reinvests the proceeds in income-producing assets. For the rest of your life, the trust pays you an income and when you die, the remaining assets go to charities named in the trust.

For example, if you purchased a stock for $25,000 and it is now worth $400,000 and you sold it, assuming a capital gains tax of 20%, you would have to pay $75,000 in capital gains tax (that is, $400,000-$25,000 = $375,000. 20% of $375,000 = $75,000), leaving you with $325,000. If you invested the

$325,000 at 8% in income-producing assets, it would provide $26,000 a year.

Now, look at what happens financially if you put that asset into an Irrevocable Charitable Remainder Trust. Instead of investing $325,000, the full $400,000 gets invested. The same 8% return will produce $32,000 in annual income. You have gained $6,000 in annual income. That's only the beginning. You also reduce your income taxes and estate taxes, plus you give a substantial amount to a charity.

So, an Irrevocable Charitable Remainder Trust allows you to avoid the capital gains when the asset is sold, get more annual income, reduce your income taxes now, reduce estate taxes later, and give a substantial amount to a charity.

What about the spouse who survives and what about the children? The income is paid as long as either spouse lives. After the death of both, however, the trust goes to the charity. Does that mean the children get nothing? Not necessarily. Proper planning can provide for them by using part of the extra money you are receiving to purchase enough insurance to give your children more than they would have had without this arrangement.

When would someone use an Irrevocable Charitable Remainder Trust? The answer is when you have a highly appreciated asset and you want a lifetime income from it without having to pay capital gains when it is sold.

An Irrevocable Life Insurance Trust The third kind of Trust that can be used in estate planning is an Irrevocable Life Insurance Trust. As we have seen, irrevocable means it cannot be changed. As the title says, this Trust involves life insurance. Under current tax laws, insurance policies you own are included in your taxable estate. Your insurance adds to your estate tax burden. The solution is an Insurance Trust. With an Insurance Trust, you transfer your insurance to the Trust. Hence, you do not own it and, therefore, your estate does not have to pay estate taxes on it.

Summary: If you wish to determine who gets the wealth you have accumulated after you die, you must make plans for your estate now.

This material is only a brief introduction to the subject of estate planning. Keep in mind that I am not an attorney. For your personal estate plan, you should consult an attorney, preferably one who specializes in estate planning.

MY ACTION PLAN: ELECTING AN ESTATE PLAN

As you now know, if you don't make proper plans, someone else will do it for you. So, no matter how little or how much you have, you need an action plan for your "estate." The amount of planning you need depends primarily on how much you have. The more you have, the more planning you need.

Step 1: Get a Will

If you have a child (or children) or assets worth more than $208,850 (that is, if you live in California; each state differs. Check the amount of the assets that can be transferred at death without going through probate in your state) and do not have a will or Living Trust, get one immediately! Technically, you do not need an attorney to draw up a will for you, but candidly, you should seek the professional services of an attorney.

If you do not have an attorney or know of one, find several by Google, preferably those who specialize in estate planning law, and call to see what they charge. Then, make an appointment with one of them. Don't put this off!

Step 2: Consider a Living Trust

Where there is a will, there is probate. Where there is probate, there are expenses. Where there is a Living Trust, there is no probate. So to avoid the cost and delays of probate, get a Living Trust. In most cases, it will cost much less than probate.

Again, if you do not have an attorney or know of one, find several, preferably those who specialize in estate planning law, and call to see what they charge. Then, make an appointment with one of them. Don't put this off!

Step 3: Think about an Irrevocable Charitable Remainder Trust

If you have a highly appreciated asset, ask an attorney about a Charitable Remainder Trust.

Chapter 11
CONCLUSION

Your personal money management should at least cover savings, budget, credit, insurance, homeownership, taxes, investments, retirement, and estate planning. The basic financial practices can be summarized as follows:

1. Save 10% and pay yourself first. "A penny saved is a penny earned" (Ben Franklin).
2. Establish a reserved account.
3. You control the budget, and until you revise it, the budget controls spending.
4. Avoid interest. The credit system can either work for you or against you.
5. Protect your assets with insurance, especially the family income.
6. Buy a house for financial reasons (tax savings and investment).
7. Put money in your pocket by legitimately taking it out of Uncle Sam's pocket.
8. Invest and reinvest the return.
9. Begin preparing for retirement early; the earlier, the better.
10. Decide who gets what's left, or the government decides for you.

Sounds simple, doesn't it? The principles taken by themselves are indeed simple, but the overall picture is complex because these areas and principles affect each other. This fact makes financial planning a complicated exercise. For example, investments have tax consequences. One investment might look like it yields more than another, but the tax consequences might mean that is not the case. The complex nature of financial planning makes seeking the services of a professional and/or professionals a prudent choice.

Be that as it may, you can master money management. The amount of your income is not the issue; it is what you do with your money that counts. David Ramsay, a Christian financial adviser, says, "What I find is that personal finance is 80% behavior. Everyone tries to fix financial problems with math. But it's not a math problem. It's not a knowledge problem. It's a behavior problem. The problem with my money is the idiot I shave with every morning. If I can get that guy in the mirror to behave, he can be skinny and rich. It's not magic" (*Success*, September/October 2006, page 40).

Ramsay is right. The amount of money you make is not the issue. It is what you do with it. Not all the superstars who make super bucks are listed among the super-rich. In 1991, there was only one. *Forbes* pointed out that while some entertainers were making megabucks, only one was among their annual list of the super-rich. That one was Gene Autry, who, at the time, was worth an estimated $300 Million. According to *Forbes,* he did not accumulate that kind of wealth by strumming his guitar but by investing. In other words, he has been a shrewd businessman who has also invested his money. *Forbes* said Autry was "as smart an investor as they come." The point is that how much money you make is not the issue. Other movie stars were making *more,* but did not end up as rich as Gene Autry.

A retired military man working at a Public School said it all when he told a friend of mine, "It's not how much money you make, it is how much money you save; it is not how much money you save, it's how much money you invest."

About The Author

G. Michael Cocoris is a gifted communicator. He can make even complicated subjects simple, clear, and practical. His breadth of experience has allowed him to relate to a wide range of audiences.

Michael received a Bachelor of Arts degree from Tennessee Temple University, a Master of Theology degree from Dallas Seminary, and a Doctorate of Divinity from Biola University. He traveled the United States for over a dozen years as a speaker. He has also been a seminary professor, visiting lecturer, and world traveler, including hosting tours to Israel and China.

Michael has pastored three churches, including a rural church when he was in seminary, an urban church, the historic Church of the Open Door, first in downtown Los Angeles and later in Glendora, California, and a suburban church, the Lindley Church in Tarzana California, a suburb of Los Angeles. While at the Church of Open Door, he had a daily radio broadcast.

Michael has written numerous magazine articles, mainly for *Biblical Research Monthly*. He has authored a number of books, including *Seventy Years on Hope Street, A History of the Church of the Open Door*; *How To Live A Biblical Spiritual Life, Clarifying the Confusion; Repentance, The Most Misunderstood Word in the Bible; Evangelism: A Biblical Approach; The Salvation Controversy; Lordship Salvation: Is It Biblical?; The Books of the Bible, the Subject, Structure, Situation, and Significant Verses of Each Book; Psalms, A Song for Every Situation, Each Summarized on One Page; and Counseling Theories, A Biblical Evaluation.* In addition, he was a contributor to The *NKJV Study Bible* and *Nelson's New Illustrated Bible Commentary*.

Michael is the pastor of the Lindley Church in Tarzana, California. He and his wife, Patricia, live in Santa Monica, California.

www.ingramcontent.com/pod-product-compliance
Lightning Source LLC
LaVergne TN
LVHW022055200926
848481LV00003B/926